THE BRANT EFFECT

HOW TO LIVE YOUR DREAM LIFE THROUGH PROPERTY INVESTMENT

IAN HALFPENNY

POWERHOUSE
—PUBLICATIONS—

Copyright

Powerhouse Publications
Suite 124. 94 London Road
Headington, Oxford
OX3 9FN

www.powerhousepublishing.com

Testimonials

"Want to know why I believe in the Brant Effect and its ability to help you build your ideal dream life through property? I believe in the Brant Effect because I knew and believed in Gary Brant. He was a principled man, full of integrity, who only ever wanted to do the right thing. Gary's stepson, the author, shares how important it is to invest your time because time is your greatest commodity. Property is a methodology, expertly used by Ian Halfpenny, to create the life of his dreams. Simply put, if you follow the guidance contained within this book, you will be able to build the life of your dreams."

– Derek Mills, Star of Think and Grow Rich, the movie,
International Speaker and Author of the best-selling book,
The 10-Second Philosophy: a Practical Guide to Releasing Your Inner Genius.

"I love success stories and learning from how people deal with challenges. Like me, the author has faced a few and tackled them full on. The Brant Effect has laid out a step-by-step guide to help you take control of your life, leave the rat race and build passive income through property investment. Passive income is not easy because if it was everyone would be following that path. However, this book breaks down strategies into easy-to-follow guidelines with top tips along the way. Follow the six steps to financial freedom to take control of your life, find balance, wealth and happiness."

– Iain Wallis FCA, Author of *Legally Avoid Property Taxes*,
#1 Best Seller on Amazon. Property Investor and Tax Strategist,
www.iainwallis.com.

"This is the kind of book I wish that I had access to many years ago. Ian does a fantastic job of laying out a step-by-step guide to achieving financial freedom through property. He challenges the status quo and guides his readers to obtain their dream life. A true from rags-to-riches story that doesn't hold back any details. This is an easy-reading guide to your future success – a must-read book."

– Tim Matcham, The Property Finance Coach, author of Amazon No.1 best-selling book, *How to Attract Armchair Investors for Property*,
www.attractarmchairinvestors.com.

DEDICATION

This book is dedicated to Mr Gary Brant, who is the very reason for The Brant Effect. The lessons and legacy from his life have given me my dream life and I pray they lead you on a journey of finding and living your dream life. He had a heart like Christ who led by example, cared for all, had a servant heart and loved everyone unconditionally. No words can describe how empty our world is without you.

To my wife, Florence, thank you for all your encouragement and support, I love you from the bottom of my heart and always will. A massive thanks to Jolyon and Lynne Barton for allowing me the honour of marrying your wonderful daughter.

To my mother, Linda, you are crazy and I love you for that. Thank you for all you sacrificed in life to raise us kids.

To my dad, David, thanks for instilling in me a strong work ethic and a hunger for success.

To my sister, Laura, thanks for being the smart one so I could be the fun one; oh, and for your pearls of wisdom throughout life.

To my sisters, Lucy and Jess, thanks for being so inclusive, loving and caring to all the family, you crazy kids.

The Brant Effect has totally transformed my life and the way I live. It gave me the kick-start I needed to get out of the rat race, escape the 9 to 5 and live my dream life.

For all my twenties and most of my thirties I was working long hours, missing out on doing the things I really wanted to do – like travelling and seeing the world, spending more time with family, taking on new hobbies and living life on my own terms. The rat race and my focus on it saw me miss important times with my family, time I can never get back. I had no freedom to do what I wanted, when I wanted as I was totally controlled by the rat race or by a boss or company that were paying me for my time. Regardless of how hard I worked, or how many hours I worked, I could never find a way of having enough money and owning my own time to invest it where I wanted to. Most of the time, I was living hand to mouth and living month to month for my salary.

I've felt the stress and anxiety that debt brings upon you; it is crippling. I've burst into tears as yet another unexpected bill arrived that I couldn't afford. I've been there, rock bottom.

I know many people who are still working hard in the rat race, being controlled by a boss, have no freedom or flexibility to be able to do what they want when they want. These people are craving more time with their family, more holidays, more time to invest in their hobbies and interests, more time to learn who they are and what they want to do, more time to make a difference in this world. They crave to own their own time whilst having enough monthly income coming into their bank account each month, with little effort. I also know many people who have escaped the corporate world but feel they are living in their own self-created rat race, still bound to exchanging their time for an income.

As a result of The Brant Effect, I am now able to live my dream life, living each day on my own terms, investing my time into my priorities. I have been able to retire from work in my thirties. Never again will I miss family events, moments that I can't get back, or adventures that I want.

This book is a detailed account of how I went from being in the rat race to designing the life I want and living in freedom. My goal is that this book gives you a clear strategy on how you too can design the life and lifestyle you love, escape the rat race (or your own rat race) and find a way to live life on your own terms, owning your own time and having the money you need.

Anyone can become financially free and there are hundreds of ways to do it. I'm going to share with you some of those and go into detail on exactly how I did it. This book is your opportunity to gain financial freedom, escape the rat race and build your dream life on your terms. Grab this opportunity and run.

Your new life awaits you...

CONTENTS

ABOUT THE AUTHOR

Growing up I was never good academically. In fact, I only have two GCSEs. One of those was in Drama, which I got a B for (and that's only because I can act the fool all day long) and the other was in Maths, which I just scraped by with a C. I wanted to be a maths teacher or an accountant when I left school, so I enrolled into the local college. I soon dropped out of college though because I found it too difficult.

I started working at the age of 11 when I had a paper round. I started washing cars at the age of 12 to get some extra pocket money before I got a job washing up in the local hotel, where I became a waiter at 15 and started full-time when I dropped out of college at 17. I certainly did not grow up with a silver spoon, I had to work hard for money.

I've just always had a strong work ethic and a drive to succeed. I've failed at virtually everything – academically at school and then at college, at all sports, definitely with DIY and at times with my finances. However, I've always had the tenacity to keep going and try to succeed.

The Brant Effect made me stop and think about life and my priorities, and showed me a new way of living. It made me realise that we are unconsciously living life backwards. Society seems to promote a lifestyle that conflicts so drastically with our real priorities and yet we just go along with it, rather than boycotting "the norm". I was trapped in the rat race, working 60–80 hours a week, with no time for family, friends, hobbies and interests. My life was controlled by a boss or company and I barely had a couple of hours each night for things that really matter.

The Brant Effect – the legacy of my incredible step-dad – has given me permission to live life in a new way, to boycott the normal way of living life, and have my priorities reflected in my schedule. As a result, I have built a multi-million pound property portfolio and been able to retire in my 30s. I have gone from nothing to living my dream life and I now have all the time in the world for family and for the things that really matter. I get to choose what I do with my time. I am in control of it, no longer bound by a boss or company.

The lessons learned from the legacy of the life of my step-dad can give you the lifestyle of your dreams too; whether that's escaping the rat race you're in or owning all your time so you get to invest it where you want. There are multiple methods for obtaining financial freedom: I chose property but you can choose whatever you are passionate about.

When I first started in property, I didn't get everything right at all. I believed a bunch of myths about property that certainly held me back. I managed to buy all the wrong types of properties when I first started investing, so, essentially, I had to unlearn everything in order to re-learn it the right way. Later on in this book, you'll hear how I went from minus £61.13 to building a multi-million pound property portfolio, which now pays my salary and income, and I will talk you through exactly how you can do it too.

Seriously: if I can do it, then anyone can. I genuinely believe that. My goal in this book is to take you on the journey, helping you to define what lifestyle you want, design it and have a clear strategy on how you will achieve it. I will detail exactly how I built my property portfolio and more importantly, built my dream life through property investment, so you can do it too.

INTRODUCTION

THE STORY

It was a couple of years ago now that I was sitting at home on a dark, grey July morning when I got the phone call from my mum.

"Your step-dad's been taken into hospital. Everything's fine; they're just doing a couple of checks," she said.

My step-dad had had an issue with his stomach for a couple of months and, with some firm words from my mother, the doctors referred him to the hospital. I could tell by my mum's tone of voice that everything wasn't really fine. So, I immediately stopped what I was doing, left work, jumped in my car, drove an hour and a half, and got to the hospital. I remember we were sitting around, trying to keep the atmosphere a little upbeat, while we waited. But in reality, behind the scenes, there was this nervous anticipation of, "What are the doctors going to say?" They'd done a couple of tests and so we were just sitting there waiting for the results, with no idea what was about to happen.

I'll never forget the moment that the doctor walked in and drew the curtains around the bed and then sat down. You could tell straight away from his body language, the tone of his voice, his empathy, that there was a problem. It wasn't necessarily the words he was saying; you could just sense it even before he opened his mouth. He sat down and told us that they'd found a number of tumours that were cancerous and they were very concerned by them. I love that my step-father's first reaction was to pray.

The news hit us all really hard because my step-father was a young, energetic, fit, strong man. So, to begin with, there was a sheer disbelief of what we were hearing. Within weeks, he had begun his chemotherapy treatment with weekly trips back and forth to the hospital. During this time he remained optimistic, positive and was a sheer inspiration in how to deal with the challenges that life throws your way. He had incredible support from people locally and all around the world. I never once heard him moan or complain, he didn't let the news or the treatment pull him down, he kept living to the extent that his body allowed. We celebrated his 61st birthday with him and he remained positive. Then, only a few months after the initial diagnosis, his health deteriorated quickly. Yet even in his weakness, he made us laugh – communicating with his eyes his pure delight as he was offered a McDonald's milkshake; he loved his food, and he would laugh along to jokes that were being told. Many people visited him at home and you could tell the impact he had on so many people and how much he appreciated seeing them. The support from Macmillan and the NHS was out of this world.

In the early hours of December 13th he took his final breath and entered heaven.

It was only after he took his last breath at home that I was able to see the incredible legacy he had left for us. I sat there with a shot of his favourite whisky and reflected on his short yet impactful life. I realised the incredible lessons his life, along with his advice and mentorship, had given us all.

He'd lived a life and a lifestyle that showed us what living was all about – but ironically, I hadn't seen it until that actual moment. My mentor may have moved on, but he'd given me this valuable lesson and what a legacy that was. A legacy that has transformed my life and can do the same for you too.

THE BRANT EFFECT

THE EXAMPLE

It was in his early fifties that my step-father was working in the rat race, working 60 to 70 hours a week, driving up and down the motorways doing 30,000 miles a year. He'd been made redundant a couple of times in the past, but this time was different. He and my mum decided that he was actually going to escape the rat race, not look for another job, but invest his time into his passions.

At the time, I found this quite controversial and confusing because my mentality and my upbringing had always been, "work hard, work long – that's what life is about." But, he gave up the rat race in order to do what he was passionate about and live his dream life.

He was an incredible photographer – of people, of landscapes, of anything really – and he has taken some wonderful pictures. He left the rat race to invest time into what he was passionate about: his photography.

As a result of turning his passion into a profession, he was able to live a life that actually reflected his priorities and at the same time make an impact through his local church and in the lives of others around him in the community.

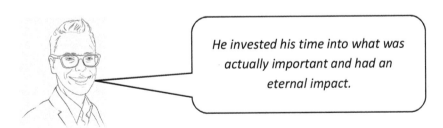

He invested his time into what was actually important and had an eternal impact.

THE LEGACY

My most important realisation came from the legacy that he left. What his life taught me was that there's simply more to life than living in the rat race, working hard and giving your family your leftover time and energy. He showed me that there is a way to live life where you prioritise the things that are important to you and live a life that you've always dreamed of. You just have to learn to tap into it, plan it, strategise it and bring it into being.

He taught me that friends and family are a priority and that living a life you love and being happy is far more important than your bank balance, your job title, your status, or even your material possessions.

His name was Gary Brant. What he taught me crystallised in my mind as what I now call The Brant Effect. His life and the lessons I've learnt from his legacy are the inspiration for this book.

His life redefined what retirement is to me. Rather than the traditional waiting until you're 65 or 67 to retire and then enjoying life and doing the things that you want to do and spending quality time with family and friends, he actually escaped the rat race, invested his time into his passions, and made a difference in people's lives from his early fifties. He chose to boycott the "norm" and I realised that everyone could do this. He showed me that everyone can have the life they want, anyone can be "living the dream."

If he'd actually lived the traditional life – the "norm" that is expected of most people – and retired at 65 to 67, he would have missed the opportunity to live his dream life. He would also have missed out on making such a positive impact on others, because he entered into heaven not long after his 61st birthday.

So, imagine if he hadn't chosen this path. Imagine what he'd have missed out on if he hadn't escaped the rat race.

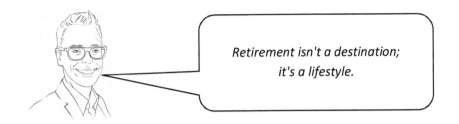

*Retirement isn't a destination;
it's a lifestyle.*

THE CATALYST

The key thing that he showed me was that retirement isn't a destination, it's a lifestyle. You don't have to wait until you hit retirement age to retire, you can retire right now. Footballers don't retire at 65, neither do other athletes, so why do we think we have to wait to retire? Even when you get to retirement, what then? It's not a destination that you arrive at, it's a new lifestyle that you embrace, so why wait until 65 to embrace it when there is a way to embrace it now.

The Brant Effect were a catalyst of change for me. It was a significant event: a specific moment in time that made me realise that, "there's more to life than this." My realisation came from his legacy and the life that he lived. It was a time where I said, "Enough is enough. Something has got to change. The life that he lived is the life that I want to live."

It was a defining moment and a significant turning point that told me: "Stop, reflect and make change." I was being pushed away from the normality of life and pulled towards a whole new way of living through his example and legacy.

I realised that being in the rat race and living the traditional life means you're actually building someone else's dream. You're building their vision and you're doing what's important to them and the company that you work for. In effect, you're sacrificing your life and your priorities to build someone else's dream. Whereas actually, life should all be about living *your* dream and having time doing what *you* want to do rather than sacrificing it for someone else's.

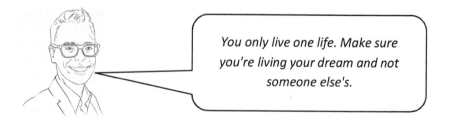

You only live one life. Make sure you're living your dream and not someone else's.

I hope that The Brant Effect will be a catalyst for change for you too. A moment in your life when you say, "Something has to change. Something has to give." You realise that you're not living the best life possible and you're not living your dream. Now is the moment that you can start to take control and start planning your escape from the traditional lifestyle and start living the life that you love.

It's when you get to this point that you realise that your priorities in life are not showing up in your schedule. What's important to you isn't getting your best energy, your time, your real attention. Instead, it's the things that are unimportant that are taking up your attention and mind space and keeping you away from the things that are important.

I always believe that things happen for a reason and I therefore believe that if you are reading this book, you have picked it up for a specific purpose. I know by following the examples that I show you and the strategies that I'm going to talk about, everyone can grab hold of their time, take control and start living their dream life. The question is, are you up for the challenge?

The Brant Effect has led me to a lifestyle that I could have only dreamed of. I could never have imagined I'd be living the life I'm living now, retired in my 30s. If I – a college drop-out – can live the life I want to live, then I know for sure that *anyone* can. No excuses. You just have to make the plans and learn the strategies and then execute them.

Your priorities in life should be seen through your schedule.

LIFESTYLE DESIGN

BOYCOTTING THE NORM

My Step-Father

My step-father was 6" 4', slim, and a silver fox. He was one of those characters who would do anything for anyone. He was the type of person that you could turn to at any point in your life and ask for support or help and he would be there to listen and offer advice. He was also the type the person, that always seemed to have two or three of everything – you could ask him for a generator and he'd just so happen to have one in his shed, bring it round and help you get everything set up.

His passions in life were photography and music. He could play virtually every musical instrument extremely well. In fact, I've now taken up lessons with his old saxophone – he would hate the sound that I get coming out of it though! He loved music and mixing and making sure the sound was right at different events.

He had such a giving nature; he would give his time to others to do whatever he could to help them succeed in life. There are loads of people who would say that he was their mentor and someone that they could turn to for support, help and advice.

I was in my mid-twenties when I first got to know Gary. He never tried to act like a step-dad, never tried to tell me what to do, and didn't try to discipline me. What he did do was take an interest and try to understand me, my thoughts, and my decisions.

I lived in Sydney for some time, and I remember this one occasion that he and my mum came over to visit. I was in my late twenties then and going through quite a tough time in life. He just sat me down and gave me some really clear, concise advice of, "You've got to move on from your past and focus on the future. These are the things that you're good at. This is what you need to focus on." He always cared about me and wanted to help, he was a great mentor to me.

By making the choice to leave the rat race, he and my mum also made the decision to sacrifice money and material possessions for living life and owning their own time. They weren't affluent at all. They placed a greater priority on time than on money and showed me that true wealth is not reflected by a bank account, but by the amount of time you own. At the time, I was so caught up in the rat race that I didn't understand the decision that they'd made. Why would you stop working and earn less money? I never understood it – until now.

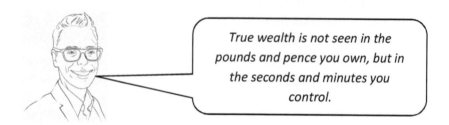

True wealth is not seen in the pounds and pence you own, but in the seconds and minutes you control.

It was literally when I sat there drinking his favourite whisky that I actually reflected and thought, "Wow. What a wonderful decision he made in his early fifties, because look what would have happened if he hadn't done that."

He and my mum would go out for the afternoon to a National Trust or an English Heritage, and walk around exploring the sights, taking pictures, having afternoon tea and doing what they enjoyed together. They'd enjoy life and do whatever they wanted to do. They would never have had that opportunity if he hadn't left the rat race in his early fifties because he would never have made it to retirement age.

At the time he decided to slow things down, my life was the complete opposite. I was entrenched in the rat race, working 60+ hours a week. My entire life was about work. So, I couldn't understand his decision initially. Honestly, I probably got a lot of my self-worth out of work. My friends and community were all in work, so why would I have wanted to come out of it? I was living the total opposite of the decision that they made to every extreme.

I was getting up at six o'clock in the morning and getting home at seven o'clock at night. I'd have dinner and have about two hours of spare time, but I didn't have the energy to do anything because I was so tired. Basically I had two hours free in my day to do what I wanted, but in essence it was two hours just to try and relax in order to get recharged and reenergise ready for the next day of work. I was commuting three hours a day to work and often working during the train journey. Trains would get delayed and sometimes I wouldn't get home until gone nine o'clock at night, have a quick bite to eat and then go straight to bed. I really wasn't living; I was just working.

My diet was awful. I didn't eat fruit or vegetables; I didn't eat much salad either. I wasn't exercising and I was 30lbs heavier than I am now. I was not fit and healthy in any way, shape or form. My entire life was about work and everything else was sacrificed for that. My quality of living was not good. I didn't have any hobbies, because I had no spare time for them. Every area of my life other than work was really poor because I wasn't giving it any time or attention it needed to flourish. Life was all about work, with two hours free to recharge.

I actually missed years of Christmases together with my family because I was so focused on my career. I lived in Australia and America for a period of time in order to build up my career and get global experience and be seen as this global professional. Without realising it, I was prioritising work over quality time with my family.

I remember one time when I was working in the rat race in Australia, I didn't have much surplus cash and my car broke down. I had $4,000 AUD in the bank. That money was earmarked to go home for Christmas to spend time with my family, but I had to go out and buy a new car and I used every last cent in my bank account for it. In fact, my card actually got declined when they were taking payment because there was $50 less in my bank account than I thought. Luckily, the car garage allowed me to re-negotiate and pay $50 less for the car.

I emptied my entire bank account to buy this car so I could get to work and back, but what that meant was I sacrificed coming home for Christmas. This would have been my first Christmas at home in a couple of years. I had no other choice because I needed the car in order to work. In fact, as I think back in life, I've missed a lot of Christmases, birthdays and celebrations, all for the sake of building a career. Missing so many important times with my family makes me feel sick now. I can never bring those moments back: I can never have those Christmases with them again, so why did I prioritise work over family?

THE PROBLEM

I was born into this world at a time when it feels like there's this social norm for your lifestyle. It's like you have to go to school, you have to study hard, you have to go to university, get into a ton of debt for that degree, then get a job and work hard – which basically means working excessive hours and sacrificing your life for work.

It feels like this norm forces you into the rat race and you're forced to work long hours, and the longer hours you spend and the harder you work, the more successful you'll seem.

The workplace even seems to encourage this. Those who work longer than they're actually being paid for are considered to be hard workers and so they get rewarded for it.

If you work in a bigger city then you're seen as more successful. If you have more responsibility or a bigger job title, then it seems like you're more successful. If you're having to work weekends, then you're considered to be really successful. It's as if your job title and the number of hours you work all of a sudden becomes your identity. The bigger the job title and the longer the hours that you work, the bigger your status and your social worth. When people ask, "How are you?" The response has to be, "I'm busy. I'm really busy." And everyone's response to that is, "Oh, good. That's really good news. You must be doing really well because you're busy."

I've actually been amazed by people's responses when they ask me the question now, "How are you?" I'm like, "Yeah. I'm chilled. I'm relaxed." Or, "I'm busy enough." People are confused by that response because it's not normal and it's not what you should answer. It's like success is defined by how busy your are or the level of responsibility that you have or how long you spend in the office. It's so easy to fall into this trap because it's the "norm". But, the "norm" is all backwards; it's totally wrong. Is status and other people's perception more important than time with your family or living life on your own terms?

The problem is that this is all at a total detriment to what is actually important in life: your family, your friends, your hobbies, your interests, your health. All of these get your leftover energy and your leftover time – if you even have any time and energy left to give to them. Before too long, you start to realise that you're missing out on life. You're missing out on maybe your kids growing up or school plays or parent evenings or you're missing quality time with your other half or you're missing birthdays or christenings. You're missing out on everything and you start to resent your job and being in the rat race. Then you fall into this period where you feel like you're trapped because you've built this lifestyle around the income that you're getting from that job. So, all of a sudden you become trapped in this vicious cycle.

I think a lot of people try to kid themselves by saying, "Well I'm working this hard and this long in order to provide for my family. Therefore, I'm doing it for my family." However, what do you really think your family want: more time with you or more money from you? A bigger house, a better car, more material things – or precious moments and memories with you?

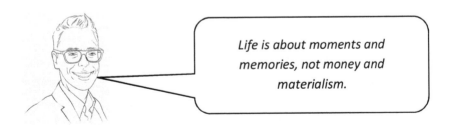

Life is about moments and memories, not money and materialism.

Now I can hear a lot of people saying, "Well, this all sounds lovely but I still need an income. I still need to be able to provide. I can't just resign from my job, get out of the rat race and do whatever I want to do." Well, what if I said that you can? What if I told you that I've found a way to own your own time, have the money that you need, and live your dream life. What If I told you that it took me just 22 months to create this as a result of The Brant Effect. This is exactly what I've been able to do as a result of The Brant Effect and exactly what I'm going to show you how to do. Clear out all the excuses in your head. You can own your own time, have enough money and live your dream life. If I can do it, then I know you can.

THE FIVE F'S

The Brant Effect and the lifestyle from it, showed me that there were five F's that were possible to have, and I wanted them:

- Freedom;
- Flexibility;
- Fun;
- Financial independence;
- Family time.

Let me explain each of these in a little more detail.

Freedom – Freedom to be able to do whatever I wanted whenever I wanted to do it. Not selfishly, but no longer to be controlled by others. I needed freedom of time and freedom from what other people thought of my career, my lifestyle and my status. I had to prioritise freedom and owning my own time above what other people think. I wanted to be living the dream, *my dream*, and not building someone else's.

Flexibility – The ability to work whenever I want, wherever I want. I wanted the ability to take a month off if I wanted to, or take an afternoon off to enjoy the sunshine, or go to a National Trust or English Heritage for an afternoon tea with my wife and family. I wanted to have a sabbatical whenever I wanted for as long as I wanted. I wanted that level of flexibility and The Brant Effect showed me that is it possible.

Fun – I decided I needed to start writing a bucket list. What are all the things I've always wanted to do that life held me back from doing and how can I start focusing on doing them? I love adventure, I love travelling, I love seeing new places and for me I wanted to have fun doing those things. I also wanted whatever work I do to be fun too; something that I was passionate about. The Brant Effect teaches us that you can turn your passion into your profession and that's what I wanted to do.

Financial independence – In order to live the dream life and own my own time, I wanted to have financial independence. I wanted more passive income coming in than our bills and our expenses. I needed to stop exchanging time for money in order to build financial independence.

Family – Ultimately, The Brant Effect showed me that I wanted to be there for my family. I didn't want to miss another Christmas. I didn't want to miss key moments – birthdays, christenings, anything. I wanted to create memories and moments that would last a lifetime with my family.

As soon as I realised that these were my goals, I had to start thinking about how on earth was I going to create a lifestyle that reflected them. I'd always been in between employee and entrepreneur my entire life, but I'd always struggled to find the balance between time and money. I'd either got loads of time but not enough money, or enough money but not enough time. I'd never been able to find that balance between time and money, until now.

A DIFFERENT PERSPECTIVE

The traditional lifestyle is to work 9 to 5 (although it's a lot longer in reality), pay off your mortgage, retire in your sixties and then you have time to do whatever you want to do. This is a very narrow focus on life and lifestyle. We have fallen victim to it and believe that is what you *have* to do, but in fact there are so many more lifestyles than just that.

Think about it. People are still working shift work – 6am until 2pm, 2pm until 10pm, 10pm until 6am. You look at European tourism and people work six months or nine months a year and then take the rest of the year off.

I know people who in their early fifties decided to sell their home, and move into a park home (which was a third of the cost), put the rest of the money in the bank and work part-time. So now they're living the life they want by making one simple decision to move. They're working part-time and they have four-day weekends, every weekend, and they absolutely love it.

I know other people who were working heavily in the rat race – 90 hours a week, flying all around the world, with no time for family or friends, very, very unhealthy – and all of a sudden, their health took a turn for the worst. So they decided, "Right. We're going to move to a foreign country where the cost of living is lower" and they took back control of their lives. Now they've got a brilliant balance and are living their own dream life.

When I worked in Australia, I discovered another lifestyle: we worked summer hours and winter hours. You'd work longer in winter and shorter in summer so you could get out of the office and enjoy life, go to the beach or take your boat out (not that I had a boat).

There's a whole new lifestyle growing where you can work from a laptop wherever you want. A lot of the pictures make it look like you can work from a desert island, but I suspect that must get very boring after a while!

In short though, there are loads of different lifestyles that are not the standard 9 to 5 rat race. People don't have to stick with the norm. There are many other options out there.

Don't get stuck into believing that you have to work in the rat race, doing long hours, sacrificing your life. There are so many other options out there.

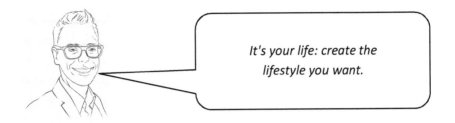

It's your life: create the lifestyle you want.

Your Key Points:

- Invest your time into what is actually important.
- Retirement isn't a destination; it's a lifestyle.
- You only live one life. Make sure you're living your dream and not someone else's.
- Your priorities in life should be seen through your schedule.
- Boycott the norm: escape the rat race and social norms.
- Life is about moments and memories, not money and materialism.
- My lifestyle goals are: Freedom, Flexibility, Fun, Financial Independence and Family.
- 9 to 5 does not have to be "the norm".
- The best lifestyle is the one that you design for yourself.

Your Action Items:

DESIGN YOUR IDEAL LIFESTYLE

We have it all backwards. We put work first and then we try to fit our life around it – that's backwards. You may be in the rat race, in your own created rat race, or simply not living your dream life yet. In order to be "living the dream" you first need to design what your ideal lifestyle looks like, then look at what work fits into the lifestyle you want and then move forward and create it.

In order to define and describe your ideal lifestyle, think about these questions:

- What's important to you?
- What are your priorities in life and how much time per week are you able to invest into them?
- How would you invest your time if you had enough money in the bank?
- What are the things that you're passionate about?
- What hours do you want to work? (You can even say zero to that, because there are options.)
- How do you want to make a difference, an impact, and leave a legacy in your life?
- What would your life look like if you had the Five F's?

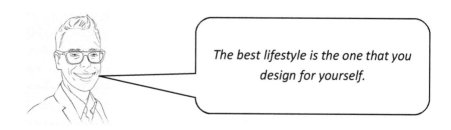

The best lifestyle is the one that you design for yourself.

Download the lifestyle goal document from
www.thebranteffect.com/resources. Complete it so you can
clearly define and describe your ideal lifestyle goals.

HOW TO BUILD YOUR IDEAL LIFESTYLE

I've always had a strong work ethic and mentality and I think that probably comes from my dad. Growing up, my dad worked very hard and worked long hours. He would be out late into the evening working. I think seeing him doing that instilled in me a very strong work ethic and a similar mentality.

Without a doubt, that work ethic came from my granddad (his father). You see my granddad was a farmer and he would wake up at five o'clock every morning, seven days a week, have his cup of tea with a couple of biscuits and then go out and milk the cows. He had a dairy farm with Friesian cows and he used to breed them, always with a Hereford bull. My granddad would take out churns of milk on his horse and cart during the war time, and deliver the milk to the nearby town. There's a picture of him out delivering the milk with snow falling all around him. I think that just captures my memory of my granddad: he was very determined and not even snow would stop him from doing the things he needed to do.

I remember my dad telling me a story about granddad which showed that he was an entrepreneur back in the day. He was explaining to my dad, "Why would I go and work for anyone else when I can buy a calf, raise it and sell it for 10 times what I paid for it in 18 months' time?" That story stuck with me and sort of worked its way into my blood. I've definitely got some of his work ethic and entrepreneurialism.

With the work ethic on the one side, I then also got wisdom on my mother's side. From an early age, I remember she would continually tell me, (and I mean *continually* tell me) the difference between being employed and being self-employed.

My mum was a bookkeeper for many years and she, like me, has got a head for numbers. (Don't ever ask me to spell anything, but you can ask me any question about numbers.) Mum's the type of person who would always put us kids first. As we were growing up, she purposely picked a job that would mean that she was there for us when we got home from school. She's not interested in materialism or possessions, and much more interested in people. She's definitely a minimalist and she's absolutely fantastic at de-cluttering anything. She wanted to be around for us as we were growing up, and even now she'll say to people that her favourite time was when her kids were in their teenage years.

The Petrol Story

I'll never forget the story that my mum used to teach me about the benefits of being self-employed. It's what I call *the petrol story*. Every time we'd drive into the local town, I knew exactly what she was going to say. There are two cars that I remember from my childhood; both were ridiculously embarrassing to be seen in. She had a Lada Samara, which was cream with a brown stripe on it – not good for street cred so I'd always be hiding from my friends – and at one point she had a brown Allegro, which was even worse for street cred. However, good family friends of ours gave it to her because she needed a car, so I really shouldn't complain. But as a teenager, it was really embarrassing being seen in either of them. Mum would never care what people thought about our material possessions. She just cared about being there for us, spending time with us, having time for us, and educating us on life.

Every time we'd drive into town we'd go underneath the railway bridge, around the corner. Then, BAM! The petrol story would begin. It didn't matter what day of the week it was, it didn't matter if it was a sunny day or if it was raining, we'd turn that corner and she'd break into the petrol story. She used this story and this journey every time to educate me. Her underlying message was: you can do anything if you put your mind to it.

As soon as we'd turned the corner and see the petrol station, she'd begin the story. Let's say petrol was £1 at the time. She'd say, "Do you know that in order to get petrol at £1, you have to earn about £1.20 or £1.30 because then you've got to pay your tax and National Insurance contribution. Yet if you have a business, and you're using that petrol for business purposes, that very £1 you can off-set against tax. So, in effect it's costing you 80p, or even less if you're a higher rate tax earner." Then she'd always just turn to us and say, "Which do you think is better: paying 80p for petrol or £1.20 for petrol?"

Well, the answer's obvious isn't it? You always want to pay the lower value. But, what she instilled in me was that creative thinking, particularly around numbers and money.

BECOMING A PASSIVEPRENEUR

With this mixture of the work ethic on my dad's side and the numbers mindset and wisdom on my mum's side, that's why I always found myself dipping in between being an employee and being an entrepreneur throughout my entire career. I've worked as an employee, I've set up businesses, run businesses, sold businesses but what The Brant Effect has shown me is that there's a way that you can own your time and money and be, what I now label, a passivepreneur.

A passivepreneur is someone who has the majority of their income purely from passive income. Passive income is money that comes to you with little or no time invested. It's money that just keeps coming in long after you've invested the time into it. For example, musicians invest time into writing music and recording songs – once that work is done, and the songs are launched, the money coming in is passive income and it just keeps rolling in.

If you continue exchanging your time for money, you will never find freedom and own your own time.

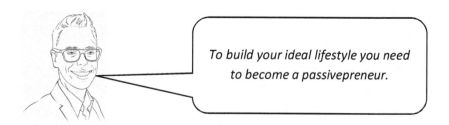

To build your ideal lifestyle you need to become a passivepreneur.

BUILDING PASSIVE INCOME

There are so many different ways that you can build passive income. Here's a few of them:

1. Invest in stocks and shares

Investing in stocks and shares is a great way to get started and it doesn't matter how much you start with. What actually matters is for you to start, monitor, review and adapt. You don't even need to research the market to learn about it or try and guess what are good investments. You just have to find an expert, a good fund manager with a proven track record, who can help you invest wisely.

Dividend stocks generate passive income, and with the right investment, you will see your money earning more money. It will take you time to see a significant return from your investment, but it's a great starting point. The key there is, "You need to be using your money to earn money. Not using your time to earn money."

2. Invest in property

There are many ways to earn passive income from property. Some of the simplest ones have great returns. You can rent out a room in your own home and earn up to £7,500 a year tax-free.

You can rent out all the rooms in your own home if you want to and turn your house into what is called a house of multiple occupancy (HMO). You can Airbnb your home when you go on holiday. If you buy a property and rent it out and have someone else manage it, then you'll be receiving passive income for the duration of that tenancy.

There are many ways of investing in property without the need to have a large deposit or any money. We're going to talk about a lot of those strategies later on in this book. But investing in property is definitely a good way to become a passivepreneur.

3. Build an online business

There are many ways of making passive income through online businesses. You can start a blog. You can build an eBay or Amazon store and systemise it and automate it so it doesn't take up much or any of your time. You can sell photos online. You can create a YouTube vlog. You can build a subscription-based education business. You can build and sell online courses.

The world of the Internet has opened up so many opportunities now, where from the comfort of your own home, with a laptop, you can create a great online business that pays you passive income.

4. Buy a business

You can buy a business with the capital that already exists in the business to pay you a salary from day one.

Providing the revenue stream is high enough within the business, you can even appoint a general manager to lead the company, which means you're investing limited time into it. It's a fantastic concept but it does take time to find the right business. There are some businesses that you would have to invest your own time into and so I'd call that more of an active-passive income.

5. Become an affiliate marketer

Affiliate marketing can be a great way to receive passive income. You partner with a company or a number of companies and you promote their products or services. For each product that you sell, or each person that you refer to them, you receive commission of what you've sold. Link this to your blog, your vlog, your website and you'll immediately have multiple streams of passive income. Amazon, eBay, Apple, Google and many other companies want to partner with people like you and pay you to refer their business.

6. Invest in peer-to-peer lending

The British Business Bank's Small Business Finance Markets report for 2017-2018 shows that peer-to-peer lending has increased dramatically over the last few years. In fact, in 2017, more than £1.78 billion was lent out to UK businesses through peer-to-peer business loans. Lending your money through a peer-to-peer company will give you a much better return than having it sitting in your bank account or a savings account.

This passive income requires very little of your time, but the returns are limited at around 6%. It's worth looking into peer-to-peer property investment lending as you can obtain higher returns – sometimes around 10%.

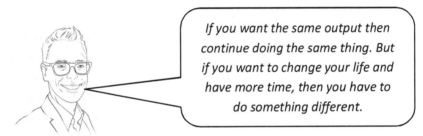

If you want the same output then continue doing the same thing. But if you want to change your life and have more time, then you have to do something different.

Building passive income will take time. It's not a get-rich-quick scheme, but it will sustain your lifestyle forever.

I've been able to build my ideal lifestyle through property investment. The passive income from property provides the five 5's I described earlier: Freedom, Flexibility, Fun, Financial Independence and Family time.

I've always had an eye for property investment and enjoyed it. I love seeing an old run-down property transformed into a modern, bright, fresh, clean home. That transformation gives me a sense of achievement and accomplishment, which drives me. When I reflected on the petrol story and understood the need to be a passivepreneur, it was obvious for me that property would be the vehicle I would use to build my ideal lifestyle.

HOW I BUILT MY IDEAL LIFESTYLE

In order to build my ideal lifestyle I knew I needed a plan, a system to follow, a course of action to take. The Brant Effect led me to create this system and following it led me to building my ideal lifestyle and financial freedom. I realised that owning my own time was far more important than having the newest, shiniest things; materialism will never make you happy and it was never going to give me the lifestyle I wanted.

The system I developed and followed to build my ideal lifestyle is called the R.O.B.U.S.T system:

- Reduce outgoings;
- Organise bank accounts and budget;
- Build up a side hustle;
- Upgrade your income;
- Save a security nest;
- Take action.

Let me talk you through each step.

Reduce outgoings drastically

I was pretty ruthless here. I looked at every expense and reduced my expenditure to the bare minimum. I then added in a few luxury items that were important to me just because they made me feel better. By doing this, I was able to find what I call my *minimum monthly financial freedom figure.*

In order to find your minimum monthly lifestyle figure, head over to **www.thebranteffect.com/resources** and download the sample worksheet there.

You have to be ruthless when you look at your expenses. Decide what is really essential and what isn't. There are many people with financial freedom who are earning a lot less money than you are. What's really important is that you prioritise the things that are actually important. The fast car, the newest TV, and a big house will not bring you happiness. Owning your own time, and investing it into the things that you want, will. Get that figure to the lowest amount possible without losing all enjoyment in life. Make sure there's a few luxuries in there just to keep your sanity.

Once you've set your minimum monthly financial freedom figure, you can then start setting your next goal: your financial independence figure. This will include a few more luxury items; maybe items you cancelled or restricted in order to achieve your minimum monthly figure. Your financial independence figure is a number that gives you a good lifestyle with no stress around income; it's not extravagant but it is more than sufficient.

The third goal is then to create your financial opulence figure. This is a monthly amount that would be far more money than you would need each month – more money than you would know what to do with – this is likely to be at least double or triple your financial independence figure.

By doing this exercise, you will have three things:

- Minimum monthly financial freedom figure,
- Financial independence figure,
- Financial opulence figure.

You'll be able to achieve financial freedom sooner if you are ruthless about reducing your outgoings. Are luxury items more important than your freedom? I'd rather own my own time than have any material possession.

Prioritise your quality of life over your standard of living.

Organise Bank Accounts and Budget

I used to handle my money the traditional way: my salary came into my main bank account and I would spend it from there. This approach encourages a month-to-month hand-to-mouth approach to your finances. I realised I wanted to get ahead of the game and not be reliant on salary coming in each month.

Restructuring my bank accounts also restructured my mindset about how I handle money and took me away from the reliance of a monthly salary. Here's how I run my bank accounts now. I have six bank accounts, each with a specific purpose. They are: Income Holding Account, Savings, Splurge, Future Salary, Investment and Main Bank Account.

Why do I do this? Because the system forces me to be wise with money. Every month you save, invest, pay all your bills and have a feel-good factor about splurging on some items without worry or consequences.

Here's how it works. All income goes into one bank account, the Income Holding Account. From there, a percentage of income goes into the following accounts: Savings, Splurge, Future Salary Account and Investment Account. You then pay yourself a salary from your Future Salary Account into your Main Bank Account.

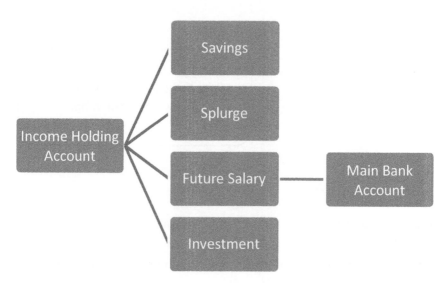

When I started this I was living hand to mouth, month to month, so 100% of my Income Account would be needed just to survive the month. After I reduced my outgoings drastically there was a little money left over, so I could implement this system. I started putting a small percentage into my Savings, Splurge and Investment accounts and the rest into the Future Salary Account. To begin with, the Future Salary Account ended with a balance of zero each month. Over time, as you drastically reduce your outgoings, build up a side hustle and upgrade your income, you will have surplus income in that account. Each month, you can then change the percentage going into each bank account and watch your Savings, Future Salary and Investment accounts build up.

The goal in this system is to start building up months or years' worth of future salary in your Future Salary Account, as you then become less dependent on your monthly income. This won't happen overnight. However, it will happen quicker than you think as you reduce outgoings, build up a side hustle and upgrade your income.

Budgeting is an essential ingredient to money mastery. Budgeting will help you implement this system successfully much quicker.

Build A Side Hustle

Building a side hustle, which ultimately can become your primary source of passive income, is essential in transitioning into your ideal lifestyle.

Start thinking through what this business could look like for you. For me, it was property investment, but for you it could be anything. What type of business would you love to launch? What could give you passive income? What could be your passion turned into a profession?

Having the end in mind first and reverse engineering is critical. Look at what lifestyle you want and then build a business around that. Some businesses require a higher level of time and energy than others; some are really hard to automate and systemise and therefore require too much investment from you. You need a business that you can outsource a lot of the work, automate a lot of the processes and systemise the tasks. What you don't want to do is create a business that is high maintenance for you, this means you are just escaping the rat race for a newly-formed rat race of your own making. My property business can be totally outsourced, which means all the income from it is passive. No time investment from myself to generate that income. Your side hustle can't be you exchanging time for cash.

Avoid building a side hustle that isn't relocatable or scalable. Your side hustle can't be a local business if you're thinking later on in life you want to relocate somewhere else. It needs to be something that you can move. You have to think further down the road – 10 years, 20 years from now – and build a side hustle that fits into your plans both now and in the future.

Once you've done that, you can start thinking about what that side hustle is and make sure that it fits into your present and future lifestyle. Remember: you've got to make sure you've designed your ideal lifestyle first, then build a business around that lifestyle.

Many people I speak to want to build a big business. When you ask them why they want to build a big business, it's because they want to sell it in three years, five years or 10 years' time. When you dig a bit deeper and ask, "Why would you want to sell it?" you find out it's because they want to make millions. You ask, "Well, what will you do with those millions when you've done that?" They usually answer, "Well then I'd live the life I've always wanted, doing the things that I want to do."

If the end goal is to have enough money to never work again and building your ideal lifestyle, then why put all that energy into building a business to sell, when you can build something that generates passive income now. It's a lot quicker to build something that will give you passive income for the rest of your life, than it is to build a business that you can sell for millions later. The idea about selling a business in three, five, or 10 years' time means I'll then enjoy life in three, five, or 10 years' time. But, there are ways, which we'll talk about later, where you can actually enjoy life now and have the passive income you need now.

Not every business will create passive income, but most can. If you provide a service, you'll have to think creatively about how you can leverage your skills in a passive way. Maybe you build a brand, you hire freelancers and you have a virtual assistant who manages the calls and schedules the service by those freelancers. As your business grows over time, you can then employ a general manager who runs it and maybe then you can just work a four-hour week at a board meeting which is more active-passive than pure passive income.

My Side Hustle

I was working long hours in the rat race with very little spare time to invest in learning and starting my journey in property. Yet at the same time, I knew I needed to invest time into building a property portfolio which ultimately would give me the freedom and flexibility I desired.

Reviewing my schedule, I found opportunities to learn more about property: I started reading books, blogs, magazine articles and listening to podcasts whilst I was on the train, walking the dog, in the gym, driving the car (not reading and driving, just listening and driving!). I basically carved out time that already existed and repurposed it by multi-tasking.

There are many free property seminars that I could have attended. However, after going to one weekend event, I realized that everything in that seminar was also in the books I had already read. I also found a lot of free information on blogs, YouTube and Facebook community groups and found that to be a better use of my time than a one-day, two-day or weekend free seminar.

I had always been interested in property and had dabbled with it in the past, but I'd never really educated myself or had a clear strategy on what to do and I certainly didn't realise it could create long-term passive income. I had some knowledge about property but found that the market and regulations had changed a lot, so I had to unlearn everything that I thought about property and re-learn it by educating myself.

Your Side Hustle

Now I realise that building a side hustle may sound totally counterproductive. If you are anything like I was, then you are probably already working long hours with limited spare time, and now I'm suggesting you work even longer hours by starting a side hustle. Yes, I understand how you might feel. But this is a short-term sacrifice in order to yield a lifetime of pleasure and passive income.

Review your schedule and see where you can multi-task; reading or listening to podcasts on your commute, in the gym, or whilst making food. Use that time to start learning about different side hustles and then start planning and strategising your own side hustle.

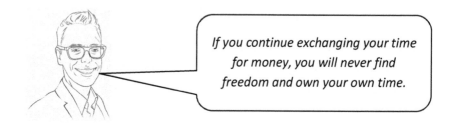

If you continue exchanging your time for money, you will never find freedom and own your own time.

Upgrade Your Income

Look at short-term ways to upgrade your income. If you are paid per hour, then maybe that's through overtime or working more hours. If you are paid on projects or commission, then can you find a way to complete more projects at work or make more sales? Is there an opportunity to obtain a bonus or increase your bonus at work, or maybe you can take on a part-time job to upgrade your income? If you're self-employed, can you increase your charges, decrease your hours, implement a new, more profitable service?

With pure determination, I'm sure you can find a way to upgrade your income in the short term.

Save A Security Nest

We've now looked at ways to reduce your outgoings, start a side hustle and upgrade your income in the short term. Any savings from reducing your outgoings, income from your side hustle and upgrade in your income will go straight into your Savings, Splurge, Future Salary and Investment Accounts, as this will start building the foundations you need in order to leave the rat race and build your ideal lifestyle.

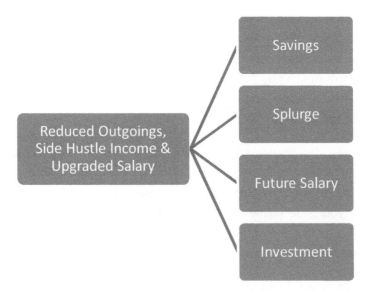

The goal now is to increase your side hustle Income and Future Salary Account to a level that allows you to leave the rat race. This means you become less reliant on the month-to-month salary from your job, as your side hustle and Future Salary Account are increasing. A point will arrive when your Future Salary Account can start paying your wage.

Focus on building up your side hustle income to replace your salary at the same time as building up your Future Salary Account to a point where it has six to 12 months of your minimum monthly financial freedom figure.

The moment your side hustle hits that figure, then you are ready to escape the rat race, as you also have the security of six to 12 months' salary sitting in your Future Salary Account. You have officially moved away from living month to month and are no longer reliant on your monthly salary from an employer.

The biggest question for you is, "How many months' future salary do you want in your account before you escape the rat race?"

You may also decide to escape the rat race before your side hustle has reached your minimum monthly financial freedom figure, giving yourself more time to focus on building up that side hustle to reach your financial freedom figure. If you want to get out of the rat race sooner, you can wait until your side hustle has created a part-time income, or your Future Salary Account can pay you a part-time income for 6 to 12 months, then go part-time at work supplementing your income with the side hustle or Future Salary Account.

Either way, by implementing these steps you're heading towards building the lifestyle that you love. Don't be disheartened if you haven't been able to cut any expenses or increase your short-term income because your side hustle will become the catalyst for saving into your security nest. Focus on building the side hustle and then you're able to set a date for leaving the rat race.

To reduce stress, I would recommend you have 12 months' income in your security nest and wait for your side hustle to be paying your minimum financial freedom figure.

Even after you've escaped the rat race, you still want to continue building up your passive income to reach your financial independence figure and then your financial opulence figure. Over time, increase your Future Salary Account so you have one, two, or three years' worth of salary there – whatever numbers you need in order to sleep comfortably at night.

This sounds so simple, right? Well, it really is. It just takes time, careful planning and focus. There will be short-term sacrifices, it will be hard work, there will be setbacks, but never take your focus off the goal. You want to leave the rat race, build a passive income and live your dream life. Short-term sacrifices are totally worth it.

Take Action

I know I'm stating the bleeding obvious here. So, let me talk about why. A few years ago before I started to build my passive income through property I spoke to a friend. Let's call this friend Alfred. I talked Alfred through all the knowledge I had learnt about property investment. I showed him how easy it was to reduce your outgoings, start a side hustle in property, increase your monthly income in the short-term, save a security nest and focus on building a property portfolio.

So, Alfred and I both had the same knowledge. Two people – same knowledge. Two years later, I now have a multi-million pound property portfolio that has enabled me to retire. Alfred, however, retained all of the knowledge and watched me do this, but never took action. Alfred is still in the rat race living hand to mouth, month to month.

Don't be an Alfred. Take action. (No offence to anyone called Alfred – I love the name enough to include it in my book.)

What steps can you take to build passive income, gain financial freedom and build your ideal lifestyle?

Your Key Points:

- To build your ideal lifestyle you need to become a passivepreneur
- If you want the same outpoint then continue doing the same thing. If you want change and to have more time, then you have to do something different.
- The R.O.B.U.S.T. System is a structured way to build your ideal lifestyle.
- Prioritise your quality of life over your standard of living.

Your Action Items:

1. Download the budget planner spreadsheet from **www.thebranteffect.com/resources** and identify your minimum financial freedom figure, financial independence figure and financial opulence figure.

2. Download "Design Your Ideal Lifestyle" document from **www.thebranteffect.com/resources** which will take you through the journey of designing your ideal lifestyle and give you clear actions steps to take.

3. Download the Deciding On Your Side Hustle document to help you define your side hustle. Download the time finder and monitor your tasks and time for 21 days. Then find the opportunities you have to repurpose your time to learn and start your side hustle.

4. Complete the "How To Increase Your Income" document and identify one way you can increase your current income.

5. Open a new savings account and label it as your *Security Nest Account*.

6. Keep reading this book.

SIX STEPS TO GAIN FINANICAL FREEDOM THROUGH PROPERTY

STEP 1 - FOUNDATIONS

Initially, I focused on 'the foundations'. I invested in property because I could see that: i) property always goes up in value over time and ii) I could create passive income and gain financial freedom quickly as people always need a home, which means there is a strong rental demand.

Property investment is active-passive, but leads to pure passive income. You've got to invest a lot of time first in learning, researching, viewing properties, speaking with mortgage advisors and educating yourself – which is very active. However, over time, as you start systemising, delegating and automating a lot of the processes you can easily turn this into purely passive income.

Here are the foundations of property investment – pillars that you must understand, research and learn before you do anything else:

UNDERSTANDING THE PROPERTY MARKET FROM AN INVESTOR'S PERSPECTIVE

The History

The property market is ever-changing. It's very different to when I first became a landlord back in the early 2000s. It seems to be that almost annually something happens that changes the property market. This is sometimes for the better, sometimes not. So, it's really important to understand the history and the rhythm of the property market.

Strategies will always have to adapt to this changing marketplace. Property, as I've said, over time always goes up. The average house price shows us this. In 1969, the average house was £4,312. In 1975, the average price went up to £10,388. (These numbers seem insignificant to us today because of inflation.)

In 1980, the average house price was £22,676. In 2016, more recently, it was £198,564. Then, as of November 2018, the UK House Price Index shows the average house price in the UK is £230,630. Here's what house prices look like in a graph from 1980 to today.

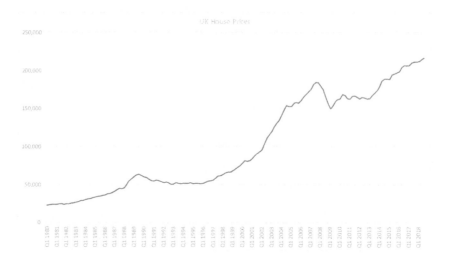

Even though there have been a couple of property crashes in the last century, the theme is clear – property prices have always gone up. Where do you think the phrase comes from "as safe as houses"?

Rental Demand

There has always been a strong demand for rental properties. Looking at the trends of housing tenure, you'll see that pre-1970s there was a huge need for rental properties. More people were renting properties in the 1920s, 1930s, 1940s, 1950s and into the 1960s than there are people renting now.

Trends in Tenture - 1939 - 2017

Renters ■ Owners

The demand for rental properties dropped from the 1970s and 1980s as Margaret Thatcher pushed for people to own their own homes. She sold the council homes to tenants and stopped the supply of council homes. The rental demand in the 1950s was higher than now, yet the current generation are being labelled as 'Generation Rent'. This generation enjoy the flexibility of being able to move anywhere, any time and rent a property. As you look at the rental market demand over previous decades right up until now, there has and always will be a high rental demand.

A recent survey conducted by the Royal Institute of Chartered Surveyors (RICS) shows that the supply of rental accommodation is expected to dwindle, yet the demand from tenants will continue to grow; as a result they expect rents to climb by 15% over the next five years.

Data eradicates fear.

Understanding a Property Market Crash

The property market goes up and down, but the overall trend over time is that it goes up. The ups and downs are just the market responding to supply and demand as well as media attention, interest rates and general economics. There have only been two significant crashes in the last century. The most recent has been 2007 into 2008, and then there was the crash in the late 1980s/early 1990s. The crash in the late 1980s/early 1990s was primarily caused by the high interest rates and the overvalued exchange rate. This recession led to a fall in property prices.

After the economy came out of the recession, house prices continued to rise well above inflation for the next 15 years. Then, in 2008, we saw the global financial crisis hit. The average UK home lost 20% of its value. The global financial crisis pushed the UK into the worst recession since the post-war recession. So, this was pretty extreme. This was caused by the banking system and a lot of deregulation.

The collapse of Lehman Brothers almost brought down the whole financial system. Property prices got high and demand dropped off, which led to prices beginning to drop. Lenders got much stricter in who they would lend to after the credit crunch, which also meant that demand started to drop. No-one can ever predict if and when the market will crash again. However, as an investor you can prepare for it by reducing your risk and exposure, and still make considerable income and wealth.

There are many ways you can prepare yourself for a property market crash. Here are just a few:

i. If you are buying property to renovate and sell it ("flipping") or building new property, then always ensure you've got a contingency plan should values drop and you are unable to sell at the price you would like.

ii. Have a Plan B that considers selling for a reduced price while still making a healthy profit

iii. For properties you have or intend to keep, ensure that you've got a positively-yielded property. Make sure that there is plenty of monthly profit now and in the future. If you have properties on a fixed rate mortgage you need to ensure there is a strong profit at the end of the fixed rate, when the interest rate goes up. If the market drops you may not be able to re-mortgage with another company and you become trapped with your current lender on the new higher rate.

iv. Ensure that you have a healthy loan-to-value on your portfolio. Loan-to-value is the amount of mortgage you have versus the value of the portfolio. Most lenders will loan 75% of the value of a property. This is much less than the 85% they used to lend before the global financial crisis in 2008. This protects the market against a crash by ensuring you're not over-exposed with your debt. A lower loan-to-value would be a further way to protect yourself, I would suggest bringing your LTV down to 65% or less to protect yourself against any potential market crash. This means prices can drop by 35% before you are in negative equity, which is considerably more than the drop during the recent global financial crisis.

You'll have to determine what level of risk you're happy to carry. No-one can tell you that. There are lenders that will lend you 85% of the value of a buy-to-let property currently, but most offer 75%. My properties saw a 20% drop in value during the global financial crisis, and this was the worst recession since the post-war recession. Therefore, I would recommend you protect yourself by having a maximum of 75% loan-to-value and further protect yourself by having a strategy to bring that down to 65% LTV.

MILLIONAIRE MINDSET

Property investment success stems from what I call a 'millionaire mindset'. Your mindset will dictate your level of income and your future wealth. If you want wealth, financial freedom and surplus, you need to develop a millionaire mindset. You've got to get your mindset right and be able to manage this before you begin investing.

Here are some of the things I did to keep my mindset correct:

Learning Keeps You Earning

It's imperative that you keep learning. Keep up to date with legislation, regulation and new creative property strategies. What worked in the early 2000s does not work now. Become a student: read as many books on property investing as possible. Keep your mind open and keep learning. A learning attitude will keep you earning and yearning for more.

The more I started to research, learn, read and take action around financial freedom, the more my wealth increased. It actually becomes a cycle of addiction. You strive to learn in order to earn. Then, the more you earn as a result of your learning, creates a yearning to earn more via learning. Did you get that!?

I've incorporated learning into my daily schedule to ensure I keep learning. I listen to a podcast when I'm walking the dog. I spend at least an hour a day on average reading and learning. When I go away on holiday, I make sure I take about three or four books with me. I don't scan-read them, I read them in detail stopping to think and reflect on what is being said.

I would recommend attending various property networking events, seminars or webinars, to learn every strategy out there – what people are doing, how they're doing it before deciding on your specific approach.

There's a lot of free information out there. Go on all the free courses you can, read as many blogs, join all the different Facebook community groups and devour the free information. All this information can help you, but remember you are reading other people's opinions, and those opinions in the Facebook groups are not necessarily from experts.

I buy virtually every property book and read it; most of them are under £20, so it really doesn't cost me that much to keep learning. I have actually never invested more than a few hundred pounds on any seminar or event, because I find there's a lot of good, free information out there that gives me everything that I need.

Rob Dix, the property author, says exactly the same, "There's no need to spend thousands on property courses. You can learn everything without doing that." I'm not dismissing the courses and I may even go on some in the future. But up to this point, I haven't needed to go on any expensive seminars because I've learnt enough methods without spending lots of money.

You can learn a lot from the people that you meet and the questions you ask them at property networking events. Every time you go to any property event, think about what information you want to know, even if it's one or two small things. Seek out the experienced people in the room that have done what you want to do and ask them those questions. Go and see the property trainers or speakers after they've done their presentations and ask them the questions. Make sure you leave each event with your questions answered.

If you want to hit financial freedom, you've got to be committed to learning.

Mentors Bring The Money

Imagine you had to drive to a nearby city, but you'd never driven a car before. Do you think you'd get there quicker by yourself or with a qualified instructor who could teach you everything? The fastest route to your destination. How to drive. How to manoeuvre. How to indicate. Hopefully you would agree that you would get there easier, quicker and with less problems and challenges with the instructor than without. It's exactly the same with property investment and becoming financially free. You could probably figure out a way of doing it yourself, but with a mentor, an instructor, you are likely to get to financial freedom quicker and with less problems and challenges along the way.

You need to find someone who has travelled the road you want to travel and follow their footsteps; someone who has faced the challenges that you're likely to face on your journey and someone who can tell you what to do to avoid or overcome them.

I've had so much free mentorship by just seeking out the right people and asking the right questions. Position yourself where you know experts will be and ask for their advice.

There are free mentors out there that you don't have to pay for, but you do have to be strategic in how you find them and meet them. Once you've joined the property groups on Facebook, you'll soon find people who have travelled the journey you want to travel. Seek out those people and be bold enough to ask if you can buy them a coffee and speak with them for ten minutes. People love talking about themselves. People love helping other people. It just feels like it's in the nature of humanity. Ask people and soon enough you'll find the right person who'll be happy to help you without having to pay a fortune for their advice.

You can also go and volunteer somewhere. There are many property businesses that would love an intern or a volunteer one day per week, five days a week, seven days a week – and just by being in the environment you will learn naturally.

Just like it's worth investing in a driving instructor, it's also worth investing in a good mentor.

Curiosity Creates Opportunity

One skill that is absolutely required in property investment, and for any entrepreneur looking to reach financial freedom, is curiosity. I've always had the sort of personality that doesn't respond well to someone saying, "You can't do that." It ignites a fire in me that says, "I will find a way and show you that it can be done, thank you very much."

Curiosity and tenacity will lead to success. I remember I was on holiday in September a couple of years ago and read something that got my mind racing. I became curious about what this person had said. Why had they said it? What did they mean by what they'd said? And if it was true, then what did that mean for me?

One sentence, in one book changed my life and set me on a journey to financial freedom that took just 22 months. How? Why? Because I was committed to learning, being mentored and I allowed my curiosity to take me on a journey, I started to question why someone had said something. I challenged my preconceived ideas and started to research what they actually meant.

Let me give you an example.

I remember I spotted this one property that had been for sale for quite a few months. I spoke to the estate agent and the reason why it hadn't sold was because it had got a low lease on it. It was a flat, a leasehold property, and most lenders will want to have at least 80 years left on the lease in order to put a mortgage on it.

This property had only 57 years left on the lease, so no mortgage company would want to put a mortgage on a property with such a short lease. The estate agent told me that it was going to cost thousands of pounds to get a lease extension.

I went on a few property forums and looked at a couple of blogs. I spoke to some property experts through Facebook. Everyone was telling me that it was going to cost me thousands to have a lease extension.

The lease extension would be an extra 99 years, so it would put it up to 156 years. I spoke to a lease expert who talked me through the process. I had never learnt about it before, but again their conclusion was that it was going to cost me thousands.

I decided to find out who the management company was that managed the service charge and was looking after the property and I called them to see if they knew what it was going to cost. I spoke to them and as far as they were concerned, they thought it was also going to cost thousands.

I then decided to do a little bit more digging and I thought, 'Well, let me see if I can find the freeholder. Who actually owns that land? Who is the freeholder that would give the leasehold?' My research led me to the company which was registered on Companies House. I was then able to find out who their solicitor was.

I phoned their solicitor and told them, "This property is for sale. It's got a 57-year lease on it. I'd like to extend the lease. I've never done this before, can you talk me through the process and the cost?"

Well, what this solicitor said just blew me away. The solicitor said that the majority of the directors in the limited company, the freeholders, still lived in the flats themselves. They felt it to be in their best interest to make sure everyone had a long lease to ensure all the values of the flats remained at full market value. In fact, a year earlier, they'd offered a new lease to every property owner and all they had to pay was the solicitor's fee, which was £420 to extend the lease.

They were not charging any money whatsoever for the lease extension. They were just charging what it was going to cost them, which was the solicitor's fee. So, I asked one more question, "Do you think they'd be willing to do that for me if I purchase the property?" The solicitor went away and asked them. He then came back and said, "Yes."

All the experts up until that point, and everyone I'd been speaking with, had told me it was going to cost me thousands. But I was able to get the lease extension for hundreds. Why? Because I was curious. I wanted to learn and I was tenacious. I kept peeling back the layers and I didn't listen to just one person. I kept asking questions and kept being curious. Three people told me it couldn't be done and it would cost me thousands, yet I wasn't willing to give up.

Later on in the book, I'll talk you through exactly how I purchased this property and what product I used because I didn't have the cash to buy it. No mortgage company would lend me the money, yet I found a way. We'll talk about that in more detail later.

I purchased that property and spent £420 to have the lease extended and now that property has 156 years left on the lease. My curiosity, despite the setbacks and challenges, made me well over £25,000 in that one property transaction.

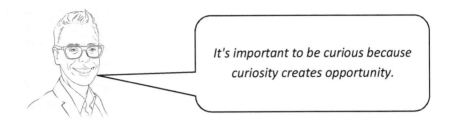

It's important to be curious because curiosity creates opportunity.

Create An Excuse-Free Zone

Excuses rob you of your dream life. They hold you back. They box you in. They create a negative environment. They do everything they can to ensure that you don't grow and thrive. They're destructive to your mind and your health. You have to create an excuse-free zone to succeed.

Now there is a difference between an excuse and a reason. The most common excuse I hear in property investment is the common assumption that you need money to make money. This is actually an excuse because as soon as you start educating yourself, you will eradicate that excuse. Later on in this book, we'll talk about how you can invest in property with no money.

Watch out for excuses that you give yourself. Challenge every single mindset. Single them out and break free of them and create yourself an excuse-free zone.

Let me give you an example. I remember one estate agent telling me that there was no way I could buy this particular property unless it was with cash. Well, I didn't have cash for the purchase but I wanted the property. I spoke to my mortgage advisor and they told me I needed to have cash to buy the property. The estate agent told me that it was going to cost a fortune to buy the property and to do the work that needed to be done to it.

I could've left that journey there with three very good reasons of why I couldn't buy that particular property, but I'd created an excuse-free zone in my life. "Find a way!" I kept telling myself. This attitude got the better of me and so I did a bit more research – and guess what? I found a way.

My excuse-free zone, tenacity, drive and stubborn determination led me down a path. I found a way to buy that property without cash and with just a 10% deposit, instead of 25%. How? I kept digging. I kept asking questions. I kept learning. I found a way.

Creative Thinking

Traditional thinking only ever leads you into the rat race and retiring in your mid-60s. You've got to think creatively to be different. You have to develop a mindset that allows you to think outside of the norm. You've got to challenge the status quo, and find creative solutions. Having the right mentor will definitely help you to think outside of the box. They will stretch you and your thinking and help you find solutions. Later on, we'll talk about many creative property investment solutions that will help you.

Your Attitude Dictates Your Altitude

You can soar high above the clouds. You can be living on Cloud 9. You can live the life you've always dreamed of – providing you've got the right attitude. Negativity strangles success. Excuses blindside you. Non-belief eats dreams for breakfast.

Your attitude has to be one of positivity, determination, tenacity, self-belief and curiosity. Whatever excuses your brain comes up with – "I'm not good enough. I can't do this. It's all well and good for that person but this isn't possible. I can't be the person that does it" – all these excuses blindside you and stop you from living your dream life.

You don't have to read much to learn that people with less education, with a poorer upbringing, with less money, with less contacts, with less anything, have the success that you've been dreaming of. There is a way to get financial freedom and yes, you can do it with the right attitude.

I remember sitting in Covent Garden with my wife celebrating her birthday. Annoyingly, I had left my mobile phone on loud and it interrupted us.

I answered the phone and it was my mortgage advisor telling me that the two properties I was about to buy, as well as the one I was re-mortgaging – all three mortgages – had just been declined. They had been due to complete within the next week or two.

Everything had looked fine. But new regulations had come out and as a result of those, the mortgage company that I had been going with had declined my application. So, there I was, in the middle of building my property portfolio, trying to be engaged with my wife and celebrating her birthday. But all that was going through my head was, "I've failed. I can't do it. That's it. This journey is over. Building financial freedom is not for me. It's not possible. All done. Forget it."

However, there was still this niggling feeling in me where my attitude was, "Don't give up. Find a way." I had to try and get rid of those feelings for my weekend, so I could actually be present in the moment. Come the Monday, I spoke to my financial advisor and said, "We just have to find a way. This mortgage company may have said no, but there's got to be another mortgage company that will say yes."

It's that attitude that then helped me secure those two new purchases and that re-mortgage by just telling myself, "Don't give up. Find a way." In this example, all I had to do was speak to my mortgage advisor and say, "If that mortgage company says no, then find another."

I've had a number of mortgage companies decline to lend me the money I need on a property – either because they had undervalued it, thought there was a structural issue, or deemed it to be unsuitable for them. I've had many knockbacks from mortgage companies. However, there is always a way. There's always another mortgage company that will lend on the property or another way to purchase it.

Giving Up Is Not An Option For You

Thousands, if not millions of people, are living in financial freedom. They're living the life that you want. They've got there because they found a system, a model, a business, something that worked well for them and they did it. They didn't give up. They worked hard. They made bad decisions. They might have had some anxiety. They might have had to deal with a bit of stress, but their determination and tenacity meant they didn't give up and they got there.

Yes, the road might not be easy, but if it was easy everyone would be doing it. You have to believe in yourself and not give up. There is a road for you to gain financial freedom and live your dream life.

Be A Property Philanthropist

Find a system that works for you. Gain financial freedom. Then help others to find a way too. Philanthropy starts local and goes global. Find a cause. Find a way of making a huge difference to one person. Then, build on that and find a way to help hundreds, thousands, if not millions of people live a better life.

Whatever you're passionate about, turn your property portfolio into a property philanthropy portfolio. Use what you have to help others. You don't have to go wild, unless you want to. Find a way to help others and make this world a better place. I personally don't think selfishness gets rewarded. I believe you reap what you sow and you can store up treasures for the future by helping people in the now.

Here's an example of what I'm doing with my portfolio at the moment to be a property philanthropist. I'll never forget this one particular guy who came to view a property of mine when I first started building a portfolio.

He'd been going through quite a difficult break up: he'd got a couple of kids and he wanted his own place so that he could provide a home for his children. However, he couldn't afford the rent for a two-bed flat in the area and he couldn't afford my flat either. He had found a new job, he was getting more overtime, he was building his career and as a result he could see that his income was going to increase. I could see that he was genuine and determined to make a home for his kids and provide for them. So, I thought: "Why not give him a discounted rent for a period of time? Why not help that one individual have a better life and provide for his kids?" So, that's what I did. I gave him a discounted rent that he could afford, in order that he could provide a home for his children.

I was speaking with another of my tenants and she was slightly distraught because her washing machine had broken down. There was water everywhere, it couldn't be fixed, it was going to cost a fortune, and she didn't have the money.

I made the decision there and then, "You've been a great tenant, you've been in the property for 18 months, you've just signed a new tenancy agreement. I'll buy you a washing machine." Why not just buy her a washing machine and make her life happier? So, that's what I did. It didn't cost all that much money in order to be a philanthropist and help.

Again, during Christmas I went out and I made a hamper for every single tenant of mine. I tailored the hamper to what I knew they would like. There were some nice ales in one of them, with some chocolates; there were cuddly teddy bears, chocolates and wine in another one – each one carefully thought through. I wrapped them all up and tied on a big bow and hand-delivered them to their front door. I purposely went round at times I knew they would be out so I could leave them on the doorstep ready for when they came home.

They're good tenants, they pay on time, they look after the properties, so why not be generous and give them a Christmas present? Property is a people business.

It doesn't have to cost much to be generous and make a difference in your tenants' lives. Over time, as my portfolio builds, I hope to do bigger and better things to help in the local community.

My philosophy is to give without any expectations in return. Be generous. That's why this book is as detailed as possible with absolutely nothing held back and no trying to sell you a ridiculously expensive course at the end of it. This book is me being a property philanthropist and sharing my knowledge to help others build a life they love through property investment.

THREE DIFFERENT MINDSETS

When it comes to property investment I have seen three different mindsets from people.

- Analysis paralysis;
- Hit and hope;
- Move and manoeuvre.

Analysis Paralysis

I've seen so many people miss out on the opportunity of gaining financial freedom for this one reason. People seem to want to know everything first; cover off every eventuality; research the most granular of detail and then some.

Let me save you years of time and speed your route to financial freedom with one sentence: "You'll never know everything." Don't be an Alfred. Alfred has spent the last two years continuing his research, analysing everything, talking to his mates about it, reading the headlines in the newspapers and he still hasn't taken action.

He's got nowhere. Analysis paralysis will stifle your route to financial freedom and living your dream life.

Let me give you an example of where I almost got caught in analysis paralysis. It was actually the first property I went to invest in. I did all my research. I got an indication of what I thought the property would be worth when it was finished because it needed some work doing to it. I could see what the property was on the market for. I went and looked at it. I had no idea whatsoever how much it would cost to refurbish that property. I found myself deep in a spreadsheet for weeks looking at everything. How much do door handles cost? How much will the hinges be? What about carpet gripper? How much is that? I spent hours trying to calculate an accurate figure of exactly how much the refurb was going to cost.

I almost missed out on this property because of my timing. However, eventually, I bit the bullet. I guessed what I thought the refurbishment cost was going to be. I went ahead with the refurbishment guessing what the end value of the property would be when it was done up and guess what? It all worked out. Luckily for you I have detailed how to get to know a property's true end value and have given you a number of case studies to help you understand how to estimate the cost of a refurbishment. You'll be far more educated than I was when I first started, so you won't have to guess your way to financial freedom through property.

I almost got caught in analysis paralysis. But here's the thing: you'll never know exactly how much it's going to cost until you start the refurbishment because as you take the tiles off in the bathroom, you don't know if the plasterboard is going to fall off as well and then you'll have to pay to have it re-plastered. You do as much planning and research as possible, but you never actually know until you move.

Hit and Hope

Hit and hope people go out there, totally uneducated, buy property and just see what happens. No research. No forward thinking. No planning. Just buy and hold. They know property goes up over time. They know it's a good investment and so they just buy one. They feel great about themselves. They've hit a home-run and they've got an investment property.

Most of the time, it's the wrong type of property and it actually holds them back from financial freedom rather than propels them towards it. I got myself caught in this trap when I first started to invest in property in the late 1990s and early 2000s. I knew property was a good investment, but I didn't want to be bored with spreadsheets. I didn't want to do research. I didn't do any education on property investment whatsoever, other than: "I can see they go up in value, therefore I'll buy one."

I went out in one week and I bought three. Luckily, my hit and hope worked, but it was purely by chance rather than an educated strategic plan.

Move and Manoeuvre

The final mindset is move and manoeuvre. These types of people are the movers and shakers in the industry. They're people like you and I who are determined to succeed. They're wise enough not to get caught up in analysis paralysis and smart enough to do enough research, get educated, have a mentor and make calculated decisions based on their business goals.

Move and manoeuvre simply means you conduct all the due diligence you can, then you take action and make a move. As you continue to learn, you continue to make decisions and manoeuvre your way through the learning, through the challenges and successes. You learn on the job. You make a decision and you continually check that decision against new information and continue to manoeuvre. You know where you're going, you have a plan to take you there and you make a move. You also realise that things change over time and you need to adapt, be flexible, and continue to check your decisions and manoeuvre your course of action when required in order to hit your end goal.

Going back to the example on the property where I almost got caught in analysis paralysis, I actually made a decision to move and manoeuvre. I moved by taking the action, putting the offer in, getting it accepted and purchasing the property. I made manoeuvres as new information came to me about the cost of door handles and the cost of gripper rods. I manoeuvred my strategy for that property based on new information that came in. If I'd got stuck in analysis paralysis, I would never have bought the property, but because I moved and manoeuvred, I was able to buy the property and make a substantial income and capital gain from it.

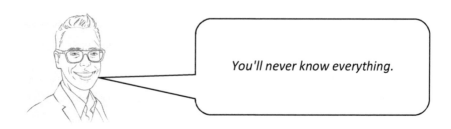

You'll never know everything.

Take action, make decisions and continue to adjust. Move and manoeuvre.

Your Key Points:

- House Prices have always gone up.
- Rental demand has been stronger than today, and it looks like that demand will continue to increase.
- Learning keeps you earning.
- Mentors bring you the money.
- Curiosity and creative thinking creates opportunity.
- You need to create an excuse-free zone.
- Your attitude dictates your altitude.
- Giving up is not an option.
- Become a property philanthropist and make a difference in the world.
- Don't get caught in analysis paralysis, or be a hit and hoper. Instead, move and manoeuvre.
- You'll never know everything.

Your Action Items:

Which millionaire mindsets do you need to adopt and which poverty mindsets do you need to ditch?

Go and buy the top three best-selling books on the three mindsets you want to adopt and read them this month.

STEP 2 - FUNDAMENTALS

MYTH BUSTERS

The second step I took to gain financial freedom was to eradicate some myths and educate myself around the following things.

Myth 1: Interest-only mortgages

I remember sitting on a sun lounger in Corfu. We'd just been celebrating my dad's 70th birthday on a cruise around the Adriatic Sea, and my wife and I had decided to stay in Corfu for an extra week. I was sitting on the sun lounger with the sun beating down on me. I was reading a book and trying to learn more about property investment and I came across a statement in the book that really annoyed me. The sentence said, "Only a novice investor has repayment mortgages."

I was outraged. How dare someone call me a novice? I'd bought and sold a few properties and I'd had a few rentals too. I thought I'd made a good bit of side hustle cash, but I'd had repayment mortgages on them. After my outrage had calmed, I realised I needed to understand why they would say this.

I'd been brought up with the mentality that you pay off your mortgage. Hence, repayment mortgages seemed as if they were essential on investment properties too. Surely. Well, it really depends what your priorities are.

As I started building my portfolio, my goal was to reach financial freedom as soon as possible by having a regular monthly passive income. So, for me, monthly income was the priority. When you have an interest-only mortgage, you are in effect taking the end profit in instalments today. So, as I was thinking about this, I had to get my calculator out to figure a few things out.

Imagine if you had a rental property worth £120,000. The mortgage company would give you 75% loan to value (LTV) and so your mortgage would be £90,000. Let's say the interest rate on that mortgage is 2%. I went to a mortgage calculator online, and found out that a repayment mortgage would cost me £381 per month and after 25 years you've paid off the £90,000.

An interest-only mortgage would be just £150 per month. Let's say that the property rents out for £450 a month. That means if you have it on interest-only, you've got a monthly profit of £300. Now, over a year that's £3,600. Over 10 years that's £36,000. Remarkably, I found that over 25 years that's £90,000.

That calculation was like a lightbulb going off in my head. You either wait 25 years and you've made £90,000 by having the rent pay the mortgage on a repayment mortgage or you have it on an interest-only mortgage and you have that £90,000 profit paid to you on a monthly basis of £300. In 25 years' time, you either have a property with no mortgage on it because it's been paid off through the repayment mortgage or you still have a property with a £90,000 mortgage on it because you've had it as interest only. This can either be re-mortgaged and extended, or you can sell the property to cover the £90,000 that you owe on it, (although you would then have to pay capital gains tax on any profit). Now remember the property was worth £120,000 but you now have 25 years of appreciation, so it's probably worth a lot more now. When I realised that I was just taking the money now rather than waiting for it later, it really got my mind racing.

Why wait 25 years to take the £90,000, when I could take it on a monthly basis now? How many properties would I need if I used interest-only mortgages to pay for this holiday? Or to pay for a car? Or to pay for my own mortgage? Or to replace my full-time income?

What about you? What could £300 a month pay for you? In fact, if you had 10 properties, all the same as this one, what would £3,000 a month do for you and for your lifestyle? That one sentence in that book that I was reading while I was sitting there on the sun lounger in Corfu changed my future forever. My goal in the next section of this book is to show you in exact detail how I did it and various methods you can use to do the same, with or without a deposit.

Myth 2: You need 25% deposit to buy an investment property

I'm still there sitting in Corfu. I now have a cocktail in my hand with the sun beating down on me and I am thinking, 'Where am I going to get 25% deposit down for each purchase? How on earth can I get 10 or 20 properties if I don't have 10 or 20 lots of 25% deposits?'

Then I remembered an old colleague of mine who shared a story with me some 12 years ago. He told me that he'd just bought a property for £80,000 and he'd spent £5,000 doing this property up. That property then got re-valued immediately at £100,000. At that time, you only needed a 15% deposit. What he was able to do within a couple of months was re-mortgage and pull his deposit straight back out again.

I thought about this story and I thought, "Maybe there's a way I could do that today. Maybe there is a way of putting one deposit into a property, re-mortgaging that property and getting my deposit back again and doing it over and over again. If there was a way, then getting 10 or 20 properties was more about timing than saving loads of deposits. Of course, I found a way and will be sharing with you exactly how I did it.

Myth 3: Mortgage free

I was starting to dream a little more now that I'd had these two revelations, and a couple of cocktails, in Corfu. What if I could be mortgage free? What impact would that have on my family? On our life? On our lifestyle? Huge, right?

There's a rise in the number of people who want to live frugally, make overpayments on their mortgage so that they can pay it off as quickly as possible, and then get on and enjoy life. It's a great concept. However, what if there was a way to *not* live frugally, enjoy life now, and be mortgage free quickly?

The common view on being mortgage free is that you have to pay off the whole outstanding debt, then you are mortgage free. But, being free of something can also mean not having the responsibility of it. Therefore, there's another definition of mortgage free – to be free of it. How could you achieve it? Well, if you have a portfolio of rental properties and the monthly profit from those properties pays your mortgage for you, then you are mortgage free – free of paying it yourself. If you want to accelerate paying off your mortgage, then you simply make overpayments by increasing the size of your property portfolio and have that passive income pay your mortgage off for you.

For me, there are two ways that you can be mortgage free: the common way where you pay it all off, and the uncommon way where you have a portfolio of properties paying it for you. As soon as I realised this, I set out a strategy on how I could build a small portfolio of properties and it only took me nine months to be mortgage free. I bet that's a lot quicker than making overpayments and living frugally in the meantime.

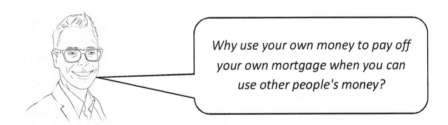

Why use your own money to pay off your own mortgage when you can use other people's money?

With a portfolio of properties going up in value each year, you're also going to be increasing your net worth. So, why pay your mortgage yourself and make overpayments yourself when you can increase your net worth and be mortgage free, all by using other people's money?

Myth 4: You lose everything when a crash happens

I was relaxing there in Corfu, pondering further. I'd heard a lot of people say that you can lose everything in property investment when a crash happens. I started to think, 'What will you really lose when property prices go down or when a crash happens?'

You see, the rent will still be coming in. The mortgage will still be getting paid. You'll still make a monthly profit. So, what do you actually lose? Well yes, you'll lose the equity and your net worth may go down, but is that the end of the world? No. Over time, the equity and your net worth will go back up again as the market rises. So, you won't lose everything.

A property market crash will only cause you a problem if you actually wanted to sell a property during the time of the crash or your fixed rate mortgage has come to an end and you can't afford the monthly payment and you are unable to re-mortgage with another company.

I realise that if I study the property cycle well enough and just wait, I can then choose to sell at the peak of a property cycle. That way round, I won't lose anything; I'll only gain. It's actually all about timing. Now, why would I sell anyway? If I have positively-geared properties that are giving me passive income each month, why would I sell and expose myself to capital gains tax?

Breaking some myths was really nice, but there was still that little voice in my head that was coming from a place of fear. Fear could have easily held me back. So could analysis paralysis. However, when I looked at the facts that property prices always go up, that there is a high rental demand, that the numbers stack up monthly to give me a profit, and that this path leads me to a life of financial freedom, that fear soon moved to one side because I was focused on the end goal of achieving financial freedom.

What I learnt in my property investment journey was that as soon as you take action and buy a property, then see that your strategy works, you will be propelled into doing it again and again. Before you know it the fear and the anxiety leave. In fact, it actually becomes a little dull rather than exciting after you've purchased a number of properties. I concluded, "The only way to eradicate fear is to take action."

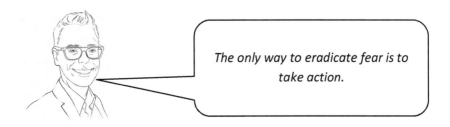

The only way to eradicate fear is to take action.

Now I know it's too easy for me to say this. I realise doing anything for the first time carries some fear or anxiety for everyone. Can you remember the first time you did something that made you anxious? Maybe it was learning to drive, or riding a bike, or a bungee jump or a skydive – whatever. Once you'd done it, that fear and anxiety leaves you. Property has been exactly the same for me and I've been through the global financial crisis. It's okay to feel the fear, but it's not okay to allow it to control you and your actions.

People believe that fear is holding them back, but actually it's a lack of knowledge, education, research and experience. As soon as I'd done the research, obtained the knowledge and education and started to buy properties, the fear soon vanished.

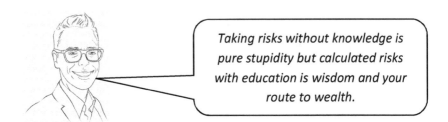

Taking risks without knowledge is pure stupidity but calculated risks with education is wisdom and your route to wealth.

Your Key Points:

- Only a novice investor has repayment mortgages.
- You don't need a deposit to take control or buy a property.
- You can be mortgage free quicker than you think, by changing your mindset on one thing.
- Why use your own money to pay off your mortgage when you can use other people's money?

Your Action Items:

Soon I am going to show you how you can buy property with no money, none of your own money or with limited resources. With that in mind, let's start visualising the journey you are on to achieving financial freedom and living your dream life.

Answer the following questions;

1. If a single-let can make £350 profit per month, on average, how many do you need to be mortgage free?

    Answer: _____

2. How many would you need to hit your minimum monthly financial freedom figure?

    Answer: _____

3. If you could buy one property every six months, how long would it take for you to be mortgage free?

    Answer: _____

4. If you could buy three properties, making £1,000 per month, every six months, how long would it take for you to be mortgage free?

    Answer: _____

5. How long would it take for you to hit your minimum monthly financial freedom figure?

    Answer: _____

Here's a simple reference guide:

6 months = £1,000 per month // 12 months = £2,000 per month // 18 months = £3,000 per month

24 months = £4,000 // 30 months = £5,000 // 36 months = £6,000 // 42 months = £7,000 // 48months = £8,000

When you work out the above, you'll be amazed at how close you already are to being mortgage free and living your dream life. Complete the sentences below:

I am _____ months away from being mortgage free (having my monthly mortgage paid for me).

I am _____ months away from being financially free (hitting my minimum monthly financial freedom figure).

Let's now look at where you can find the money you need to achieve the above.

Download my Route to Financial Freedom Through Property document on **www.thebranteffect.com/resources**.

STEP 3 - FINANCES

The third step on my journey to financial freedom was to learn how to manage money and establish a healthy relationship with it and understand how money actually works.

MONEY MASTERY

I feel it is really important to talk about money for a brief section. Why? Because, as you invest in property, your monthly income will go up. Your net worth will also go up. But, if you have a poor relationship with money, this won't actually help you; in fact, it could make things worse.

Before I invested in property, I had a negative net worth and I wasn't very good with mastering money at all. I remember when I was 19, my mum and dad sat me down. The stress, pressure and anxiety of my debt was just crippling me and I kept sweeping it under the carpet as if it didn't exist. The debt felt huge and all-consuming, but my parents sat me down and mentored me. They helped me plan my way to controlling it and creating a plan to get out of debt completely, which actually concluded in my dad buying my car off me and my mother coaching me monthly.

I set up glass jars in my wardrobe, each one with a category of what I could I spend my money on. Each month, I would put a budget in those jars and I could only spend that amount each month. That lesson and that overwhelming stress of debt, along with the system I set up and the mentorship from my parents, shaped my relationship with money forever. Measuring your net worth is really important and it has helped me make much better financial decisions.

Emotional purchases, no clear budgeting, burying your head in the sand over your finances, are all habits that need to be resolved first. Managing your money by using different bank accounts and allocating the money into those sub-categories will help you take control of your finances.

There's a template on **www.thebranteffect.com/resources** to help you budget and measure your own net worth.

Money mastery matters if you want to be financially free and live your dream life. It's absolutely pointless trying to create wealth and financial freedom if you're useless with managing money. You have to change your relationship with money first. "More is better," is a myth. Money won't bring happiness, and materialism won't buy happiness.

In fact, every financial milestone that I've hit has been a total anti-climax, which makes me realise it's not about the amount of money you have; it's about living a life you love through owning your own time. Time is the most precious commodity and being able to invest it where you want to is the most valuable thing anyone could ever have. For me, The Brant Effect has taught me that real wealth is not about your net worth, your bank balance or material possessions. It's about owning your own time and being able to invest into what really matters – your passions, people and your priorities and giving back and helping others. That's where true happiness and real wealth are found.

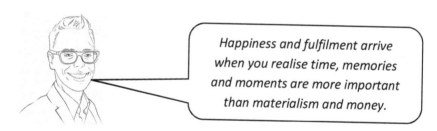

Happiness and fulfilment arrive when you realise time, memories and moments are more important than materialism and money.

The B.I.A.S.E.D. SYSTEM

There are a lot of great books on money mastery and the subject is far too big to go into real depth here. However, here are some ways I have mastered money. It's called My B.I.A.S.E.D System.

B – Budget

I have a spreadsheet that goes back nearly 20 years and I can tell you exactly what I've spent my money on. I budget everything. Every week.

Every month. It's budgeted. I know what I can spend my money on and I know what I can't spend my money on. With a budget, you can control your expenses and manage your money. It stops you forgetting about expenses, burying your head in the sand or ignoring it. I've always budgeted treats too, small items that make me feel good about my financial situation. Sometimes this has been simply one very nice cup of coffee a week, other times it's been more. I've learnt to be happy with a little or happy with a little more through budgeting.

Having a budget creates a stress-free way of living. If the spreadsheet says, "No," then it's a no! Monitoring and analysing my expenditure, and adapting things accordingly before I get into trouble, has given me a stress-free way of managing my finances. Every expense is planned and forecasted on the spreadsheet. It stops you from accidentally going overdrawn and spending more than you have. My sister has a budget breakfast meeting schedule in her calendar; time to purposely monitor, analyse and adapt her budget.

I – Investment

You have to send money out and let it come back bigger and stronger – like a boomerang. Let money work for you. Send money out, by investing it, and let it come back to you bigger. Property is great for this, but you can also do things on a smaller scale. A friend of mine has started to invest in vans; converting a van into a camper and then selling them on. He doubles his investment every time. It's time to let money make you money and release yourself from exchanging time for money.

A – Avoid bad debt

There's good debt and there's bad debt. Good debt is debt that is used for an investment: for something that will go up in value or generate income both in the short-term or long-term. Bad debt is debt that is incurred to purchase items that depreciate in value.

Mortgages that buy property that goes up in value and gives you a passive income are therefore good debt. Clothing and cars that depreciate in value are therefore bad debt. I went through many years without even having a credit card as this removed the opportunity to have bad debt. If you don't have one, you can't use one. If you've got one, then use it wisely to build up your credit score but never buy something you can't afford – because if you can't afford it now, what makes you think you can afford it later with the credit card interest added onto it?

S – Save

It doesn't matter how much, but it matters about getting into the habit of putting money into a savings account each month. There have been times when I've saved pennies and others where I've saved a lot more. It's more about creating that habit of saving. Giving yourself a safety net for unforeseen expenses stops you from going into debt and reduces financial pressure and stress. Little steps can improve your financial situation dramatically. It's well worth the effort.

E – Evaluate everything

Every week, I review my finances and evaluate them. Am I investing in the right things? Have I spent too much in one area or not enough in another area? I never allow myself to bury my head in the sand. I confront and evaluate my finances weekly. Evaluating actually decreases stress and subconsciously helps you make wise decisions when you are out shopping or being tempted by something, because you know exactly what you can and can't spend your money on. You are in control and that feels good.

D – Delayed gratification

Delayed gratification is a saviour. I've learnt that most of the time you can have whatever you want but maybe not when you want it. If you can't afford it today, don't buy it. Just wait and buy it later. It may even be cheaper later, but most of the time the delay will actually take away the desire or highlight the fact that it's not a good purchase in the first place. If it is an essential purchase, then budget and plan for it.

This B.I.A.S.E.D system focuses me to save, invest, think ahead and even allows me to enjoy some treats each month. The amounts don't matter to begin with; it's about building a process and a system that works.

Your Key Points:

Money mastery matters if you want to become financially free. It's pointless earning more if you can't handle it.

Happiness and fulfilment arrive when you realise time, memories and moments are more important than materialism and money.

The B.I.A.S.E.D system will help you master money.

Your Action Steps:

Take action now by downloading my budget and forecasting spreadsheet from: **www.thebranteffect.com/resources**.

Start implementing the B.I.A.S.E.D system now.

Mastering Money Helped Me Go From Minus £61.13 To A Multi-Million Pound Portfolio

After living in Sydney, New York and then Boston, I decided to finally move back to the UK. I remember I moved from Boston to London with just £1,000 in my bank, free accommodation for two weeks, no job, no decent or recent property knowledge to draw upon and no plan whatsoever. I had two houses that had a tiny bit of equity in them, but they were still rebounding from the property market crash. I couldn't pull any of that money out. I had nothing. I was at rock bottom and had to build myself up.

How did I go from £1,000 in my bank to a multi-million property portfolio with passive income paying my salary and allowing me to retire?

Well, the first year was a total write-off year. In fact, I went backwards. I got a job and spent all the money I earned on living in London. I invested nothing and so after 12 months in London, I'd gone from £1,000 in my bank to –£61.13 in the bank. I know the exact amount because of my budget spreadsheet that I reconcile with my bank weekly.

I knew I needed to manage money better and get control of it. My mindset around property had been a hit and hope one. I knew property was a good investment but I didn't know what to do. I obviously had no money and I'd never heard about no money down property investment.

So, I did what I knew. I cut my expenses and started saving for a deposit. I moved out of London to Abingdon, which saw my rent half. That straight away went into my savings. I made a couple of other sacrifices and was able to save a little bit more. I stupidly didn't even invest in any property education. I didn't read any books, blogs or listen to any podcasts. I just did what I knew, which definitely slowed down my journey to financial freedom. In fact, at the time I hadn't even heard of financial freedom and didn't know what it was or anything about it. I just knew it would be a good idea to get back into property investment.

The only way I knew to make money in property at the time was to have it as a side hustle and add value to a property. So, I started looking around for a property that needed some work doing to it. Within 12 months of moving out of London, I had saved enough for a small deposit and managed to purchase a house that needed some work doing to it. I moved into it, kept saving, and spent the savings monthly on doing up the property slowly. It took over a year to fully renovate it.

I sold the property – just before my step-dad was diagnosed with cancer – The Brant Effect changed my mindset from making money in property to wanting to build a passive income through property so I could have the lifestyle I loved. The Brant Effect and the profit from this one property then propelled me into building a portfolio and gaining financial freedom. In essence, I took the six steps to building my ideal lifestyle that we discussed earlier. I reduced my outgoings, started a property side hustle, increased my short-term income at work, set up a security nest account (which I used to invest in property), focused on property renovation and took action. This then gave me a lump sum to begin building my portfolio, though not enough to buy my financial freedom, so I needed a strategy to help grow that money further.

PROPERTY STRATEGIES

Let's look at some of the property strategies you can use to help increase your finances and build your ideal lifestyle. Then I'll talk you through, in granular detail, the specific strategy I took to build my portfolio and gain financial freedom in just 22 months and the steps that you can take to do exactly the same.

Rent A Room

One way that you can earn money from property is to rent a room. Do you know that you can earn £7,500 a year tax-free, currently, if you rent out a room in your house? It's the Government's rent-a-room scheme. That's one quick way to change your life straight away by earning an extra £7,500 tax-free.

Flipping Property

Here's another way of earning more tax-free cash. In this tax year, you can earn £11,700 tax-free through capital gains. So, if you and your friend, business partner, husband or wife buy a property together, improve it by adding value and sell it, you won't pay tax on £23,400 of the profit. The allowance is 'use it or lose it'. You can't carry it forward into the next year.

If you rent a room out and have one project where you flip a property each year, you can have an extra £19,200 a year coming in to you tax-free.

One property I purchased had been on the market for quite some time. When I met the seller I asked him about the property and he told me that it had been sold for £103,000 six months previously. However, as the surveyor came out, they'd found damp in the property. They got a builder's report and a number of quotes, but the people buying it had decided to pull out. He'd then put it back on the market and had no interest, and so had reduced the price and then reduced the price again.

I asked him what he needed for the property and as a result, I was able to secure that property for £74,000. I spoke to a number of builders and I got the damp treatment done for £5,000 and then sold the property quickly for £105,000. Minus solicitor's fees, stamp duty and a couple of other costs, that project made just over £20,000. It was nothing major, but as I did it with someone else it was completely tax-free. So, why not use your tax allowances each year? Later, I'll talk you through exactly how to find properties like that and finance them.

How To Buy Property With No Money Or Low Money

When I moved from London, the only way I knew you could buy property was to save a deposit and get a mortgage. It's the only way I knew because it's the only way people had told me. I hadn't educated myself about property investment, I hadn't read any books or listened to any podcasts, I just knew what society had taught me. I was amazed to find out that there are many ways you can buy property with no money or with a low amount of money. Isn't that amazing!? You can actually buy property with no or low money.

Here are some of the ways you can buy property with no or low money.

Lease Options

Lease options aren't easy, but they are very powerful and used correctly they can create a win-win solution for you and the seller.

"What is a lease option?" I can hear you asking.

It's a legal agreement that allows you to take control of a property, generate income from it and have the option to buy it at a later date. You'll agree with the owner a monthly payment which would cover their mortgage and associated costs, a purchase price, the length of the agreement and an upfront payment. Yes, you need to pay an upfront payment but in some cases this can be as a little as a pound. Some level of money exchange is required for it to be a legal agreement.

Let me give you an example here. A seller can't sell their property on the open market. Maybe they're in negative equity or there aren't many buyers interested in their type of property; maybe they've lost their job and can't pay their mortgage and they don't want the perceived hassle of renting it out themselves. You approach them and suggest a lease option. Let's say the house is worth £100,000 in today's market and their mortgage and associated costs are £250 a month. You agree a lease option to buy the property for £100,000 in three, four or five years' time and to lease it from them for £250 a month up until the date you purchase. Let's say they have no equity in the property, so then you pay them £1 for the lease option. You pay them £250 a month to lease the property from them, you then find tenants who pay you the market rent of £575 per month, and as a result you have a gross passive income of £325 a month coming in. No money down, no deposit, no credit checks, no mortgage required and then in three, four, five years' time you have the option to purchase the property at the £100,000 agreed, (note it may be worth more at the end of the lease option). If you are paying £100,000 for it now and it's worth £120,000 when you exercise your lease and purchase the property, then you have just made £20,000 in equity on top of the monthly income you've been receiving.

The one pitfall you have to watch for in this strategy is where you are going to get the money from for the deposit later on. If the market hasn't increased by 25%, which it probably won't, then where is this money going to come from? You'll need to plan and strategize for that. Bridging finance may be a good option for reducing the required deposit.

Bridging Finance

Bridging finance is a fantastic option used in the right situations. Imagine – and this does happen a lot – that there is a property with a market value of £100,000. It's been on the market for months and no-one is interested in buying it. In fact, they've dropped the price to £90,000 then they've dropped it to £80,000 and there's still no interest.

With bridging finance, you can buy this property with no money down if you have an offer accepted at £70,000. There are bridging lenders out there that will lend you 70% of the market value of the property regardless of the actual purchase price. So, the bridging company will come out and value it at £100,000; they will then lend you £70,000 to purchase it.

At this stage all you need to cover is the solicitor's cost and stamp duty. However, you can then re-mortgage this onto a buy-to-let mortgage. A buy-to-let lender will give you 75% of the value – the LTV (Loan to Value). With a £100,000 property, that means they will give you £75,000. So, as soon as you re-mortgage this with a buy-to-let mortgage, you then have £75,000 to pay yourself back the solicitor's fees, (which were probably about £1,200), the stamp duty, (which would have been £2,100), and then pay the bridging finance back their £70,000 and any fees.

Once you've re-mortgaged the property onto a buy-to-let mortgage you will have 25% equity in the property, which is £25,000. it's probably making you around £300 to £400 a month in passive income and it cost you zero. Nothing. Zilch. That's the power of bridging. People regularly talk about ROI (return on investment) and what yield you're getting for your money. Well, with this strategy it's infinite return on your money. Just think about it one more time. Zero in... £25,000 and £300 to £400 a month out.

Would you like to know how I bought a flat for £925 last year using bridging finance? Earlier on, I talked about a property that needed a lease extension. The estate agent told me I couldn't get a mortgage on it. The mortgage advisor told me I couldn't get a mortgage on it. Even if I did, then I'd need a 25% deposit. I used bridging finance to secure this property and then converted it onto a buy-to-let mortgage.

Let's look at the numbers on this one. I purchased it using a bridging loan. This particular company gave me 90% of the purchase price. So, I didn't need a 25% deposit, I just needed a 10% deposit. The moment we exchanged contracts, I had the lease extension complete. The property purchase price was £68,500. The mortgage amount was £61,650, so I had to put in a deposit of £6,850. The solicitor's fees were £1,200. Stamp duty was £2,055 and the lease extension cost me £420. So, my total cost was £72,175.

Purchase Price	£68,500
Solicitor's Fees	£1,200
Stamp Duty	£2,055
Lease Extension	£420
TOTAL COST	£72,175

Mortgage	£61,650
Deposit Required	£6,850

After we completed, I contacted the buy-to-let mortgage company and they came out to value the property. They valued it with the new lease at £95,000. On a buy-to-let mortgage, they would lend me 75% of its market value, which was a total of £71,250.

New Value	£95,000
New Mortgage	£71,250
Pay off old Mortgage	£61,650
Balance	£9,600

Let's go back over the figures: it cost me £72,175 and they gave me £71,250. So, at the beginning I put £10,525 into the deal – which was the deposit, solicitor's fees, stamp duty and the lease extension:

Deposit	£6,850
Solicitor's Fees	£1,200
Stamp Duty	£2,055
Lease Extension	£420
TOTAL	£10,525

The £71,250 from the mortgage company paid off the bridging loan of £61,650 and gave me £9,600 back. So, I purchased a two-bedroom flat, which now makes me £300 a month and has £23,750 equity in it, for a grand total of £925. After three months of renting it out, it cost me nothing. A free flat!

Here's an example of sending money out to make it stronger when it comes back to you. I sent out £10,525 and it gave me £9,600 back in cash, £23,750 in equity and £300 a month rent for the rest of my life. This whole process took me three months. That's how to use bridging to secure property for little or no money down.

Property is a great vehicle for sending money out and making it come back to you bigger and stronger.

Buying With Other People's Money (OPM)

Another strategy for buying property with none of your own money is to use other people's money. There are thousands of people with tens of thousands of pounds of savings in their bank account, all getting about 1% or 2% interest. If they're lucky, they may have locked it away for a few years and be getting 2% to 2.5%. Maybe they found a great scheme even for 3% or put it into the stock market and they're getting a 4% or 5% return. What if you offered these people 5%, 6% or even 7% return on their money? This is exactly what peer-to-peer lending platforms are doing, but usually lower than 7%. What if they give the money directly to you and you returned it to them with 5%, 6%, or 7% interest? That's a win-win solution. Right? They are getting more money, because you are offering them a higher interest than they are currently getting, and you're getting to use their money to make more money.

Sounds lovely, but where do you find these people? As you start learning and building your knowledge, you'll soon get to a point when you know which strategy you are going to follow. Once you're at this point, and remembering that property is a people business, then it's all about getting your message out there. You're going to help maximise their return on investment through your knowledge of property. To get your message out there, I would recommend doing the following:

i – Join every Facebook property community you can find and start telling people who you are and what you do. The more people that know, the more people that can refer others to you.

ii – Go to as many property networking meetings as possible. Tell people what you do. In these meetings you'll find property sourcers, who are people that source and sell property deals, many investors, and also people who are thinking about investing because they have the money but don't necessarily have the time or the knowledge. These people are looking for people like you – someone who is committed to building their knowledge, learning the right strategies and willing to make serious money in property. They are people who have no spare time or desire to learn more about property, but they do want a better return for their money than the banks are giving them right now. You can offer them a totally hands-off solution, which is exactly what they're looking for.

iii – Friends and family. You may have friends and family members who have some money in savings or in equity and are keen to invest but don't know how. You can join forces with them and help their money earn more by giving them a better return on their investment.

iv – Go to property auctions, not to buy property but to network with the people who are there. At property auctions, you will find people who are interested in buying property but don't have the knowledge you have. These people are potential joint venture partners: you can work together to make money through property, with their money and your knowledge.

A word of caution with this strategy: you have to ensure you can return the money and have a contingency plan with the person if for some reason you are unable to refinance and pull all your money out of the property. That plan can be that they get the monthly profit from the property to pay any shortfall in returning their money or a share of the equity left in the property.

Why would you want to use their money? What are you going to do with it and, more importantly, how are you going to return it? Let me talk you through a property purchase I made recently as if I'd done it using other people's money.

This property had been on the market for months. I'd made an offer on it and the owner had declined it. I went back a few months later, noting that it was still for sale, and I put in exactly the same offer again. Things had changed for them. They'd received no interest in the property and so they finally agreed to sell it to me at that price.

This was a one-bedroom flat that I secured for £55,000, which needed a little bit of cosmetic work doing to it. Here's how this deal would have worked out if I had used other people's money. There are many ways I could have purchased it, but let's say I purchased it though a buy-to-let mortgage – one that would have allowed me to do what's called a *further advance* on the mortgage after six months of ownership. You put down a 25% deposit, which would be £13,750, plus you pay the solicitor's fees of £1,200, as well as £1,650 for the stamp duty, and then this particular property cost £4,000 to refurbish it so the total outlay £20,600.

Purchase Price	£55,000
Deposit @ 25%	£13,750
Solicitor's Fees	£1,200
Stamp Duty	£1,650
Refurbishment	£4,000
TOTAL MONEY IN	£20,600

Let's say that I'd agreed to use someone else's money on this property. I agree to give them a 7% return on their investment within 12 months. I would need £20,600 from them for the purchase and I would agree to give them back a total of £22,042 (including the 7% interest after 12 months). To ensure the refurbishment costs are accurate and don't increase, I would ensure I have a builder quote for all the works required prior to making an agreement with my joint venture partner for the money. Alternatively, it may be worth considering asking for a contingency fund of £2,000 should the refurbishment costs increase; a fund I only draw upon if needed and I return with 7% interest.

After the refurbishment, I rent out the property and it makes £365 profit a month. After six months, I approach the mortgage company and ask for a further advance. They come out and re-value this property at £85,000 and lend me 75% of the new valuation. That's £63,750. Now remember, the existing mortgage is 75% of the purchase price of £55,000. So, that's £41,250. My further advance is £63,750 minus the existing mortgage of £41,250 and therefore they transfer £22,500 to me.

Now, if I'd used an investor's money for this property, then I would still need to pay the investor back their money plus interest, which would be £22,042 and that would leave me with a grand total of £458 to reward myself with.

Re-Mortgage Income	£22,500
Pay Investor Back	£22,042
TOTAL BALANCE	£458

That's how you can buy property using other people's money whilst at the same time giving them a much better return on their money.

New Value	£85,000
New Mortgage	£63,750
Pay Off Old Mortgage	£41,250
Balance	£22,500

This property transaction took a total of nine months from the moment the offer was accepted. In the first 12 months of ownership, this property has given me £21,250 in equity and £365 a month in passive income, and gave me more money back than I put into it to begin with.

How many £365s per month would it need to pay your mortgage? How many would it need for you to become financially free? How many £21,250s in equity would you like to increase your net worth? You're probably thinking, 'Where do I find properties like this?' Well I will tell you exactly how I found that one and many others shortly.

Let me tell you how I actually purchased this property to give you more ideas of how you can do it too. I realised that my wife and I had two very nice cars, but they were depreciating assets so we decided to sell both of the cars, which gave us the funds we needed to make this property purchase.

The monthly income from that property now pays for a lease on our cars. We then used the further advance money to buy a similar property. Both of those properties now lease two very nice cars for my wife and I. In the process, we have sold two depreciating assets and purchased two appreciating assets (properties). Both of them have made us over

£20,000 in equity each, and we now have the monthly profit paying for us to drive around in two brand new cars. We could have chosen cheaper cars, but I'm a petrol head and my luxury item to myself is my car.

100% Development Finance

Another no money down strategy can be to find land with planning permission and project manage the build of a new house or a small number of properties. There is a rise in lenders who will lend you 100% of the funding you need to build a property or small development. They make their money by splitting the profit with you. This is sometimes 50% each; others I've seen have been 60/40 in their favour.

With this strategy you don't need any money to begin with, you just need to manage the project and collect the reward at the end of it. If you go down this route, then you need to have a contingency plan should the properties not sell. I would ensure the project has 25% profit in it as a minimum and that you are building something that will be rentable because then, if the properties don't sell, you can obtain a buy-to-let mortgage on them and keep them. You'll have to work with the development financing company to build a suitable contingency plan.

Equity Release

If you currently own a property, you may be able to release some of the equity (money) in the property. Your current mortgage provider may offer you a further advance or second-charge mortgage, or you may be able to re-mortgage with a new provider, using this money to then begin your investment journey to being mortgage free and financially free. With interest rates being so low at the moment, it isn't likely to cost you much to release equity. I've been able to release equity and save money on some properties by re-mortgaging them on to better deals. This could be a low or no money down option as it's not costing you much to obtain the money.

Pensions

Another way to fund your property portfolio could be through your pension. There are two types of pensions that you can use as a vehicle for your property portfolio. A SIPP or a SSAS.

A SIPP is a Self-Invested Personal Pension and it allows you to choose your own investments and manage your pension pot yourself. With a SIPP you are able to use your pension fund to invest into commercial property. Currently a SIPP allows you to borrow up to 50% of the net fund value for the purpose of purchasing commercial property.

A SSAS is a Small Self-Administered Scheme which allows you to control your investment through a limited company. A SSAS can lend your business money, buy land or buy property. Managed well, and you could pass the money and property down the generations in a tax-efficient way.

Using your pension pot to invest in property can be one way of beginning your property journey. (Disclaimer: I am not a financial adviser. I highly recommend you seek advice from a financial professional who can talk you through the advantages and risks of a SIPP or SSAS before you do anything.)

STEP 4 – FORMULATE STRATEGY

Now you've got the foundations right and developed a millionaire mindset. You've studied the fundamentals for property, improved your financial knowledge and seen how some property strategies can help your finances. It's time to formulate a strategy.

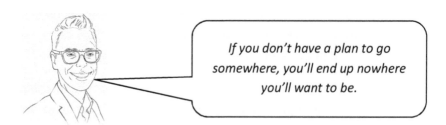

If you don't have a plan to go somewhere, you'll end up nowhere you'll want to be.

I didn't have a bottomless pit of money and I knew the money I did have I needed to maximise, as there wasn't enough to buy all the properties I needed in order to reach financial freedom. I researched all the different property strategies and concluded that this one was the best for me, and for most people starting off in property and wanting to build financial freedom through property. I purposely haven't covered all property strategies as it's very overwhelming and could leave most people in analysis paralysis.

I scaled my property portfolio through the BFF-RRR strategy. This is the strategy I dreamed up while sitting on that sun lounger in Corfu, and I used it to build my portfolio and gain financial freedom. As I continued to learn, I found out that most people in the property world call this the BRR strategy. However, I found that BRR doesn't full explain the step-by-step process required. I'll talk you through the strategy here, but go into granular detail in the next section of the book.

- B – Buy.
- F – Finance.
- F – Fix up.
- R – Rent.
- R – Refinance.
- R – Repeat.

Buy, Finance, Fix up, Rent, Refinance, Repeat is the BFF-RRR Strategy. The one-bedroom property we just talked through was purchased using this strategy.

B – Buy

You source and find the right property to buy. For that one-bedroomed flat, I purchased it because I could see that I could add value to it and that is critical. It was the same with the property that needed the lease extension. That lease extension added value to the property. You have to source something that you can add value to.

F – Finance

Then, you need to finance the property. We purchased this with a deposit from selling the cars and a buy-to-let mortgage. However, you could have easily used other people's money for this purchase, your own savings or bridging finance.

F – Fix up

You then fix it up: this is where you get the opportunity to add value. Adding a new kitchen or updating the existing one doesn't cost all that much. It's the same with the bathroom. Before you make an offer, make sure you can add value to the property. It's essential that you find a way of pulling all or the majority of your money back out of the deal and that is only possible if you add value to the property.

R – Rent

Then you rent it. The rental income becomes your passive income. It's the funds that pay your financial freedom figures and gives you the lifestyle you want. We'll talk about how to find the right tenants later, but in this strategy we are looking to hold the property and rent it for the long-term.

R – Refinance

Once all the works have been completed, you want to be able to refinance, gain a further advance or place a second-charge mortgage on the property so you can pull out all your money.

R – Repeat

Finally, you repeat. As soon as you have pulled your money out, you want to use that money again to buy the next property. You continue following these steps – Buy, Finance, Fix up, Rent, Refinance and Repeat – until you've hit your financial opulence figure.

Your Key Points:

- Mastering money helped me go from –£61.13 to building a multi-million pound property portfolio.
- You can buy property with no deposit, none of your own money or with little money.
- I bought a two-bed flat for £925 last year and you can too.
- You could be paid £458 to buy a one-bed flat using none of your own money and make £365 monthly for the rest of your life.
- Property strategies to consider: Rent a Room, Flipping Property, Lease Options, Bridging Finance, Other People's Money, 100% Development Finance, Equity Release.
- BFF-RRR has been my BFF.

Your Action Steps:

Before we look at each of these steps in granular detail, take action now by completing the strategy definer at: **www.thebranteffect.com /resources**. By completing this document, you will have a clear idea of which property strategy you want to focus on and where you are going to finance your portfolio from.

STEP 5 – FOCUS AND EXECUTE
THE BFF-RRR STRATEGY

Now is the time to start focusing on your strategy and executing it. Let's look at what properties to search for, how to finance them, how to fix them up, how to rent them out, how to conduct the refinance and then repeat the whole transaction all over again.

B – BUY

What is the right property to buy? Here's the model I use to ensure I'm buying the right properties: The C.A.T.C.H.E.R. Model.

C – Cosmetic

The properties you are looking for need only cosmetic work. Nothing structural; nothing major. You'll look to improve the kitchen, the bathroom, a bit of painting, replace the carpet and a few finishing touches. Maybe just a little damp work to sort out too. You're looking for quick fixes. No big extensions, no major works allowed.

One property I recently purchased looked awful. The kitchen was tiny; it was difficult to manoeuvre around. The lounge had this awful bright wall. The bathroom was a bit rundown. There were massive holes in the wall, which looked like someone had just fallen down the stairs and almost gone through it. The entrance was this bright orange colour, so it made the approach to the property look horrible. It was just awful.

Well, that type of property is perfect. Why? Because structurally it was sound; it didn't need any major work doing to it. It just looked horrible. It had been on the market for months. They'd reduced the price a couple of times and still no-one was interested in buying it.

When I viewed it, I could see its potential and I worked out the refurbishment costs. So, I asked the owner that one simple question, "What do you need for the property?" You see property is about creating a win-win solution for both parties. It's not about screwing down the price to the lowest level. You have to be ethical, honest and honourable. I secured this property for £76,000. The refurbishment cost me £4,640 and it's now valued at £110,000. With stamp duty and solicitor's fees taken out of it, I've made £25,880. I've pulled all my money back out and the property is now making just over £350 a month. I will talk you through the refurbishment, with the pictures of this property, later on in the book.

A – Add value

You need to be able to add value. So, you're looking for a property that's ugly, horrible, disgusting, maybe unliveable or has a low lease. You need to be able to add value to a property, in order to be able to pull your money back out again. If you are unable to add value, then walk away. It'll delay your journey to financial freedom as your money is trapped in there waiting for the market to increase before you can release it. What a waste of potential that is.

T – Thirty Percent Below End Value (BEV)

As a quick rough guide, the property has to be around 30% below end value (BEV). If I can see its end value, which is post-refurbishment, is going to be £100,000, then the maximum I'm likely to want to pay for the property is £70,000. That's 30% below its end value (BEV). Why? Because, this gives me enough margin to pay for the solicitor's fees, stamp duty and a typical refurbishment. If I can see that I can obtain the property at 30% BEV and I'm able to add value to it, then I know I am likely to be able to refinance and pull all my money back out of it again. If the property doesn't need much work, but I can obtain it at 30% BEV, then I also have the option to purchase it using bridging finance and potentially none of my own money. I'll still need the solicitor's fees and stamp duty. When I'm searching for properties, I use this quick guide to tell me if it's worth investing more time into further research. If I can see there is a potential to purchase 30% below end value then I know it's worth viewing the property, so I can estimate the refurbishment costs and then spend more time analysing the deal further.

C – Close to amenities

This is really important. I only buy properties that are walkable into a local town or an area that has all the amenities that people require – banks, supermarkets, shops, coffee stores, bars, restaurants, schools and public transport are essential. This broadens your tenant pool. Buying a cottage in the middle of nowhere will be painful to rent.

H – Highly motivated to sell

Most of the properties I have purchased have been from people who are highly motivated to sell. Highly-motivated sellers are people that need to sell and don't just want to sell. Typically, they are selling because:

- It's a probate property.
- They're going through a divorce.
- They're relocating.
- The property is being repossessed.
- They've been made redundant.
- They're a tired landlord.

These highly-motivated sellers are looking for people just like you – people who can give them what they need to proceed with a sale quickly. They really don't want to be in a chain; they want to get rid of the property as soon as possible.

E – Excel Evaluation

I don't purchase any property unless it successfully passes my Excel evaluation. I assess all the numbers related to the property to ensure it is the type of property I want to purchase. There are two key areas I look at: what do I need to purchase it for in order to be able to pull my deposit back out again, and what will the monthly profit be from the property?

To decide on the first, I look at the end value of the property (what will it be worth post-refurbishment?) then I look at all the costs involved in purchasing and renovating it: solicitor's fees, stamp duty, mortgage fees and the renovation costs. The total purchasing cost can not exceed 75% of the end value price. For example, if my total purchasing costs are £75,000, then the end value must be £100,000.

Looking at the monthly profit for the property, I review the mortgage cost at the purchase price and how much it will rise to after a re-mortgage, the running costs of the property, letting fees, service charge, ground rent and any other fees, and then minus that from the rentable value of the property. The goal here is to ensure that it is making at least £300 per month, post re-financing.

If I can't get my money back out again, or the profit isn't at least £300 per month then I walk away.

R – Rentable.

There must be a high rental demand for the property. But how will you know? What I did was to phone around all the estate agents in the town where I invest and ask them one simple question, "What type of property could you immediately rent out because there is a shortage in supply and a high demand for?" This then helps me target my search for properties that I know will have a high rentable demand. Ask a number of estate agents and you will soon find a theme.

Where Will I Find The Right Property Geographically?

Before I decided on an area to invest in, I looked at a number of things across 10 different locations. What is the average cost of properties in each area? What is the average rent for those properties? What is the average profit for each property and the deposit required? I didn't look at the cheapest areas in the cheapest towns and cities. I wanted good areas that attracted good tenants.

I conducted this analysis on 10 different locations – towns and cities – and I put them in order of which was the least amount to purchase and the highest monthly income. I then selected the area I was going to invest in.

Now, this area wasn't the highest rental profit – in fact, on average it was £25 per month less than the best area. Also, the type of property I was looking to purchase was not even the cheapest in the UK, (in fact, on average it was around £10,000 more than the cheapest area). So, why did I go for this area to invest in? Because of lifestyle. It was within five miles of my home. I don't want to be driving up and down the motorway, viewing properties, dealing with builders, dealing with letting agents, tenants and problems. My time is far more important than a little bit more profit here and there. So, I chose to invest locally and put my lifestyle first. You may not be able to do so. Therefore, I would encourage you to find a great letting agent who will be able to deal with everything for you. Over time, look at hiring a local person who can view potential properties for you to purchase; have them video when they are walking around the property for you. I recommend doing that after you've purchased a few properties, so you know what you're looking for.

I would also recommend you pick one area and stick to it, because then you really get to know the prices in that area and you can spot the deals quicker. You also only need to have tradespeople in that one area which makes life a whole lot easier. There were many areas where I could buy properties for £50,000 up to £120,000 that fitted the C.A.T.C.H.E.R. model and would make a minimum of £300 to £400 a month. So, I set £300 a month as my absolute minimum for a monthly profit, post refurbishment refinancing.

During my research, I noticed that for the BFF-RRR strategy to work I needed to focus my search on two types of properties. Flats that were £50,000 to £70,000 and renting for £450 to £525 a month, and houses that were £70,000 to £90,000 renting for £575 to £625 a month. I also noticed that terraced properties were achieving £400 to £480 profit and had a high rental demand. If I went below £50,000, then the property either wasn't good for the rental market or it didn't fit the C.A.T.C.H.E.R model, and if I went above £90,000 then the profit wasn't as strong or it was hard to get all your money back out again.

It's really important to be clear and focused on what type of property you are looking for before you start your search. There are a lot of good property deals in the market and it's too easy to get distracted by them. Focus on one strategy and one type of property first, this level of focus breeds success.

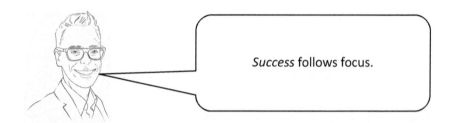

Success follows focus.

EXACTLY HOW I DID IT: FINDING THE RIGHT PROPERTY DEAL

Online Portals

I'm not going to over-complicate things here. There are a lot of people who will tell you that you need to write a letter to every house in the area that you want to buy on a certain colour paper and with a certain colour pen. You then market your way to finding a motivated seller – with leaflets, flyers and advertisements. This strategy works; I'm not knocking it. However, I did something far simpler than that. Every property I have purchased, following my C.A.T.C.H.E.R model, I have found on Rightmove or Zoopla. Yes, you read that right. Nothing too fancy, nothing too difficult: I just used the Internet to help me find them.

Let me explain how I used these portals to focus my efforts on only viewing the properties that I thought would have a highly-motivated seller behind them. Zoopla has the best functions for searching. If you type in the area that you want to search, along with any other data that you want – the price, the number of bedrooms, the type of property (you can leave those blank if you want to) – if you then click on the "advance search" options you can sort the order of the properties.

You can sort them into "most reduced" and it will show you the percentage the property has been reduced since it was first on the market. This is valuable information. As I look at this search now, I can see a page full of properties in my local area that have already been reduced by 20% or more. These properties tell me that there's likely to be a highly-motivated seller behind them or at least a story behind them. It's enough information for me to get interested.

On Zoopla, you can also search into "most recent" or "most popular". If you search "most recent" and then you go to the very last page, these are the properties that have been on the market for the longest. Again, there is potentially a highly-motivated seller behind them. If you do the same with "most popular" and you go to the last page, these are the properties that no-one else is interested in – they've got low popularity. You may even notice a property or two that has been most reduced, been on the market for a while and has low popularity. These are great properties to start researching further. If you click on the property and scroll down in the property details, you will see the price history section. This tells you when the property was first listed and each and every price drop, the date, the amount and the new asking price. Again, valuable information.

What I then do is jump over to rightmove.com and I find the same property on there. I click on it and if you scroll down you'll see a section that says, "Properties sold nearby" or "Market information." Click on either of these and look at the sold prices for similar properties in that same street or area. What you're looking for here is to get a rough idea of what its end market value will be post-refurbishment.

Ideally you want to find exactly the same property, same size, similar layout, with a modern kitchen, bathroom and cosmetically looking good as that will tell you what its end market value is likely to be. If the numbers are stacking up, and it looks like you're not too far off the 30% BEV (below end value) then I look at a website that gives you all of the sold prices for all of the properties in that street. Rightmove just gives you a selection, a few.

The website is www.gov.uk/search-house-prices; there is also an app called 'Sold Prices' which pulls the data from the website. Fill in the details there and start looking for an exact property that matches yours. The website doesn't show you pictures, which is really annoying, so when I've found a similar property (e.g. terraced house, three bedrooms) and I can see the sold price I then Google the exact address to find pictures of the property, which are normally then found on a different page within Rightmove or on Zoopla. Then you're able to see the exact price it was sold for and see the pictures of the exact condition it was in. I use this method every time in my research.

The first property I found using this method was a three-bed terraced house. I noticed on Zoopla it had been reduced from £115,000 down to £105,000 and then further to £95,000, all in the space of four weeks. This was all on Zoopla. I then looked at Rightmove, the Sold Prices app, and the Government website to find similar properties that had already been refurbished. These refurbished properties had sold for £120,000 to £125,000. So, straight away I knew the end value was likely to be £120,000 to £125,000, if I could match the quality of finish seen on these others.

Thirty percent below end value (BEV) is £84,000 to £87,500 and it was now on the market for £95,000. So, we're not too far off what I think I need to purchase it for and what the owner is asking for. At this stage, I don't know the full refurbishment costs for the property, so it hadn't passed the Excel evaluation yet. I could see that it needed some work doing to it, but it definitely fitted the C.A.T.C.H.E.R model. So I went to see the property.

I asked the one simple question to the owner, "What do you need for this property?" They told me, and the following day it was all agreed through the estate agent and I purchased the property for £87,000. It got re-valued at £125,000 and the refurbishment cost I estimated at £5,000. When I came to re-finance the property, I wasn't able to get all of my money back out again. I had to leave a few thousand pounds of my own money in the property, but the rental income profit has given that money back to me many times over now, so it was worth purchasing.

A word of caution. Just because it's advertised for a certain amount of money, doesn't mean it's worth that amount. You have to look at what properties have really been sold for. What are people actually willing to pay for those properties? Estate agents will often put something up for a far greater value than its real worth and then look at reducing it by 5%, 10%, or 20%. So, not every property that's been reduced by 20% is the right property to buy. That's why I suggest you focus on 30% BEV (below end value).

Most of my properties have come through this method of sourcing. What I've learnt is that highly-motivated sellers will still go through a traditional estate agent to sell a property because that's what they know. When I look at why people have sold their properties to me, they fall into one of the following categories:

Relocation

They were relocating area – either to somewhere cheaper or work was paying for the move – or they were relocating and were intending to rent in the new area. What I've found is that their motivation to relocate is higher than their desire to obtain the top value for their property. They want a quick sale and to move on with their life in the new area.

Divorce

People going through a divorce tend to be splitting the money between two parties; they also tend to be more focused on getting rid of the property and moving quickly than they do about obtaining full market value. I have found that being able to offer a quick sale with no chain to a divorcing couple has greatly helped them obtain the money they want so they can move on with their lives. You've actually helped them.

Moving abroad

People who are moving abroad also tend to want a quick sale, as they are more excited about the move and starting their new life abroad than they are about getting top value for their house.

Repossession

The final type of property that I've purchased has been where a repossession is pending. One of the properties I've purchased was about to be repossessed, but it had been placed with an estate agent on Rightmove. It was on the market for a few months, they had already done a couple of price drops, so I went to view it and asked the magic question, "What do you need for the property?" We agreed the sale immediately as the property fitted the C.A.T.C.H.E.R model.

ESTATE AGENTS

Working with estate agents and finding the properties through Rightmove and Zoopla has been the way I've sourced the majority of my properties. You need to build trust when working with an estate agent – never cancel a viewing, never withdraw an offer and always phone them when you say will. If they trust that you will deliver, then they will come to you with property deals. I've had estate agents phone me before other investors to tell me about vendors who have a property that they need to sell quickly. Why would they do that? It's because I've built up trust with them and they know that I will complete. So now the deals start coming to me. I don't withdraw and I complete as soon as possible, so for them it's just one phone call and a potential quick sale.

This sort of thing happens when you start to walk around the estate agents and let them know what you do. Most of them will have heard all of this before so be confident, honest and tell them exactly what you're looking for. I went into all the local estate agents and said, "Hi. I've just moved to the area and I'm looking for properties between £50,000 and £120,000. I'm in the market for a few but they must be close to town, need some work doing to them and be something that I can rent out – maybe through you – when the work is completed. Do you have anything like this?"

Why did I say £50,000 to £120,000 when I've just told you my ideal properties were £50,000 to £90,000? Well I still wanted to have the opportunity to see the other properties just in case they fitted with the

BFF-RRR strategy and make the right monthly income, even if they are over my price range. I may also be able to negotiate them down a little to be within the range. You get the estate agents' attention when you know exactly what you're looking for along with the fact that you want a few. I then asked them the following questions to try and help identify the properties that I would be interested in.

There are six questions:

Q.1 – Are there any sellers that are on the phone to you every day asking for an update? Which property is it that they are selling?

Q.2 – Are there any properties that you have very little interest in?

Q.3 – Do you have any properties that are on the market with you and another agent?

Q.4 – Are there any properties that the seller has said that they need a quick sale for some reason?

Q.5 – Do you have any properties that are both for sale and for rent?

Q.6 – Are there any empty properties that you have on the market?

What I'm doing is trying to identify which properties are likely to have a highly motivated seller behind them.

SOURCING HIGHLY-MOTIVATED SELLERS THROUGH MARKETING

The estate agent method works, but it's very proactive. If you want an inbound marketing strategy where motivated sellers are phoning you directly, then you need a marketing plan to grab these people's attention. There are many ways to source motivated sellers through marketing.

Here are some of them:

Method 1 – Word of mouth.

Speaking to people, every single person that you come into contact with, and telling them what you do certainly helps. Not just because they may be or they might become a highly-motivated seller, but also because they might know one. So, it's vitally important you tell people who you are and what you do.

Only last week, I was at one of my properties meeting with the tenants and one of the neighbours came out to me, as I was getting into my car, and said, "Ian, you asked me to give you first refusal if I ever sell. Well I'm having to move; would you be interested in purchasing my property still?"

This happened purely because I told her what I did. In fact, the very property where I was meeting the tenants, I purchased directly from the owner because he knew exactly what I did and wanted a quick sale so he could move abroad.

Method 2 – Newspapers.

Advertising in the local newspaper will build your brand and have motivated sellers phoning you directly. If you go to the classified section in your local newspaper, and even in some national papers, you're likely to find an advert that says, "Sell you property fast. Money waiting. Call us now." These are investors who are looking to provide a fast solution to the seller's problem. They are likely to be using 100% of other people's money to buy the property with cash or they have a deposit and a bridging company ready to purchase quickly. After the purchase they will then transition the property onto a buy-to-let mortgage. Whatever method they are using, they have highly-motivated sellers phoning them directly.

Method 3 – Leafleting.

Have you ever had a leaflet through your door? Leafleting the area that you want to purchase in is another way of finding highly-motivated sellers and having them call you directly. I have heard many people say that it must be on yellow paper with red writing as it gets the best results, and as this is a tried and tested method I'm not going to argue with it. I would say that leafleting needs to stand out and over time the red on yellow will become so familiar that people won't even read it. I would also ensure that you don't put your leaflets through with the local paper, as there are already too many leaflets in there and it's easy for people to grab all of them and throw them straight in the bin. You want to have someone deliver it when nothing else is being delivered.

Method 4 – Website.

It doesn't take much time or money these days to secure a good domain name and build a professional-looking website. Tell everyone about your website, use Google AdWords to help advertise it to find motivated sellers and ensure you have a strong call to action on it so people will get in contact with you.

BUYING THROUGH AUCTION

This strategy works for a lot of people. However, it hasn't worked for me. I have found auctions to be too competitive, which has resulted in people paying too much for a property. That's just my experience but don't let that put you off. Go to an auction and see what properties are selling for.

Make sure the numbers stack up in order for you to pull out your money and if they do, then you know auctions could be an option for you and your strategy. Ensure you speak with your mortgage advisor and solicitor beforehand on how to best secure a property through auction, as you'll need to put a deposit down on the day and complete within 28 days.

The balance when you're starting out is going to be between time and money. It costs time to build up a relationship of trust and tell people what you do via word of mouth: spending time working with estate agents and networking. Whereas leafleting, advertising and having a website will cost you money. You have to decide which is right for you.

Your Key Points:

- Use the C.A.T.C.H.E.R model to ensure you are buying the right property.
- Don't buy a property unless you can add value to it.
- Emotional purchases will hurt you financially.
- You need to find your area for investment before buying any property.
- Know exactly what type of property you are looking for.
- Finding the right deals can be simple using online portals, estate agents and word of mouth.
- There are many motivated sellers out there who want to sell you their property for a bargain price.

Your Action Steps:

Decide now where you will focus your geographic search by downloading the goldmine area spreadsheet on: www.thebranteffect.com/resources.

What approach will you use to find properties? Online portals? Estate agents? Marketing? Word of mouth? Leafleting? Newspapers? Websites?

Answer: _____

Assess every property through the C.A.T.C.H.E.R model and ensure it passes the Excel Evaluation. Download the C.A.T.C.H.E.R and Excel Evaluator - Deal analyser.

BFF-RRR

F – FINANCE

Where To Find The Money

One of the biggest barriers that holds people back from property investment is money.

When I first started to think about property investment, I only knew one way: that was to save for a deposit and then buy a property. The idea of building a portfolio of properties sounded great, but I thought it would take me a lifetime to save deposits each time. This is a common misconception that you need a lot of money to buy property.

You may not even need to find the money as there are many strategies you can use to buy property with little or no money. Let's explore some of the options you can consider for finding money for building your property portfolio.

- Do you have assets you can sell to raise funds, like my wife and I did with our cars?
- Can you follow the six steps I took to build my ideal lifestyle and reduce your costs, organise your bank accounts, build a side hustle, upgrade your income, save a security nest and take action. This will enable you to save an investment fund ready for build your property portfolio.
- Can you release equity from your own home or other assets you have?
- Can you invest in property through your pension by setting up a SIPP or SSAS?

If none of these are an option for you, then you automatically know that your finance strategy is going to be joint venture partnerships, helping others maximise their return on their money by using your knowledge of property, or no money down property strategies.

No Money Down

We've talked about finding properties that are genuinely 70% below their true end market value and using bridging finance to fund them.

Going back to the previous example of buying a property for £70,000 when its true market value is £100,000, the process for securing this type of property is for you to have a bridging finance lender value the property at its true market value of £100,000. They will then lend you £70,000 (70% of its market value) to purchase the property. This method enables you to put no money down in order to purchase the property.

Why would the lender do this? They secure a loan of £70,000 on a property valued at £100,000, so, for them, they feel safe and secure knowing there is 30% equity in the property. Residential lenders offer 90% and 95% of a property value, which is a much higher risk than this example.

Lease Options

We've talked through lease options earlier on in the book, so I won't go over it again here in too much detail. Importantly, lease options do not require any money upfront – well, maybe just £1, as to make the lease option legally binding, money needs to be exchanged.

Other People's Money

You can use other people's money, as I described earlier in this book. People are currently getting 1% to 3% (if they are lucky) from their money in savings accounts. You can offer them 6% or 7% return on their investment, and use that money as a deposit to purchase a property following the C.A.T.C.H.E.R model, refinancing it to pull the money back out of the deal, and give it back with the interest agreed added to it.

Joint Venture

A joint venture is when two, or more, people come together and share their knowledge, experience and finances for mutual benefit. When I worked in the corporate world, I had some savings and could have used that for property investment, however I didn't have the knowledge or the time.

Imagine if I had met someone who had all the property investment knowledge and time, but didn't have the money to invest. What a great partnership we could have had. There are many people with money but without knowledge and time, likewise there are many people with the knowledge but without the money. Bring these two parties together and you have a 50:50 joint venture partnership, both bringing equal value to the table for a property deal. You don't need to have money in the bank in order to buy a property, you can use the C.A.T.C.H.E.R and BFF-RRR models along with a joint venture partner's money and buy property, both equally benefiting from the profit in the deal. Knowledge is just as valuable as money.

PROPERTY SOURCING

With your new-found knowledge, you could become a property sourcer, finding properties that are below market value or 30% below end value, and selling those deals to other investors, charging them a healthy fee in the process. Save these fees, and after a handful of them, you will have enough for a deposit to begin your journey using the BFF-RRR strategy.

Low Money Down

I've talked you through an example where I had to put 10% down, rather than the traditional 25% deposit required for an investment property. I invested a total of £10,525, and £9,600 was returned to me within a few months. How did I do that? I found a lender who would offer either 75% of the open market value of the property, or 90% of the purchase price – whichever was the lowest.

I don't know your situation in detail, but what I can say is that there is definitely a way you can start building a property portfolio, whether you have a little or you have a lot. Just keep rereading the sections above and start searching for suitable properties and investors and you'll soon be on the road to financial freedom.

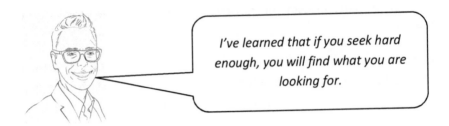

I've learned that if you seek hard enough, you will find what you are looking for.

MORTGAGES

Mortgages are obviously part of the finance that you will use to fund a property purchase. There are hundreds of mortgages out there, but there are three types of mortgages that I have focused on in building my own property portfolio. When I first started buying my portfolio, I had just gone self-employed with no day job at the time, so I had no proof of income – none. That doesn't have to hold you back. There are many mortgage companies that will lend you money with no proof of income. Why? Because they are lending it based on the property, not based on you. The property is income generating. When it comes to a buy-to-let mortgage, how much money you are earning does not equal how much money they will lend you. Lenders look at the property income not your personal income.

Lenders each have their own calculation about what they will lend you on the property and they will conduct what they call a "stress test." They want to ensure that as time goes by and interest rates rise that the rental income will still cover the mortgage payments. What they want to see is that the rent is at least 125% of the mortgage cost. Some require 135%, whereas the majority of lenders will want to see that the rental income is at least 145% of the interest-only mortgage.

To further complicate things, they also test this at a higher interest rate. They want to see that the rental income still covers the mortgage if interest rates went up to 5% or 5.5%.

For example, if you have a property that is valued at £120,000 and your mortgage is £90,000, 75% LTV. Here's what rental income the lenders would be looking at;

Interest Rate	125%	135%	145%
5%	£468.75	£506.25	£543.75
5.5%	£515.63	£556.88	£598.13

A lender looking at 5% / 125% stress test would want to see a rental income of £468.75.

Whereas a lender wanting to stress test at 5.5% / 145% would want to see a rental income of £598.13.

Lenders will therefore dictate the amount of rental income they want to see from a property in order to give you a mortgage on it. You will not only need to consider this when you purchase the property, but you will also need to ensure the calculations work when you are re-financing the property too.

Buy-To-Let Mortgage

All three of the mortgage products I focused on in building my portfolio, all ended up on a buy-to-let mortgage and these mortgages require that you have 20% to 25% equity in them – which means the mortgage lender will lend you 75% to 80% LTV. The goal in any property purchase is to add value to it – by doing so, you are making money on the capital increase of the property as well as the rental income.

By adding value to the property, it will enable you to re-finance and pull out your money. A buy-to-let will allow you to do this after six months, whereas a bridge-to-let and refurb-to-let will allow you to do it quicker.

With a buy-to-let mortgage product, there are a number of lenders that will allow you to do either a further advance or second charge after you have owned the property for at least six months. This is called "the six month rule". Both a further advance and second charge are an opportunity to pull equity out of the property. After six months, you ask them to come out and re-value the property, knowing that you have added value to it. They agree on a new valuation and they lend you 75% of the new valuation.

Remember the flat I purchased for £55,000. I obtained a further advance on that property after six months and it got re-valued at £85,000 because I'd added value to the property by refurbishing it. Let's look at those numbers again.

Purchase Price	£55,000
Deposit – 25%	£13,750
Mortgage – 75% LTV	£41,250

The new mortgage amount is £63,750, this is the maximum amount they are willing to lend on the property as it's 75% of its £85,000 value. I already have a mortgage with them of £41,250, so they were willing to give a further advance of £22,500.

The risk with using a buy-to-let mortgage and a further advance, is that you never know what the final valuation is going to be until the surveyor comes out after you've owned it for six months. You've done your research, you have comparisons in the same street or nearby, but it's all about what the lender's surveyor agrees it is worth on that day. The following two mortgage products do not carry that same risk.

Bridge-To-Let

The second type of mortgage I focus on when building my portfolio is a bridge-to-let mortgage product. This product costs a little bit more, but it allows you to pull your money back out faster and gives you the certainty of the end market value before you have purchased the property. You purchase the property using bridging finance, add value to it by doing a refurb and then immediately convert it onto a buy-to-let mortgage. Recently, I've done this with a property purchase and it took a total of three months to pull out all of my money, which was longer than anticipated. Depending on the lender, you'll find that his transaction will normally take four to six weeks.

This is basically two products in one. It's a bridging loan to begin with that then converts into a buy-to-let mortgage. The bridging loan is charged on a monthly basis and is usually around 1% of the total loan amount, charged monthly. For example, a £50,000 bridging loan at 1% is £500 per month. You can either pay for this monthly or add it to the loan. The valuation fee for this product is higher too, as they are doing two valuations in one; they are valuing how much it is worth today, and how much it will be worth when you have refurbished it. Expect to pay around £500 for a valuation fee.

Your mortgage advisor may also charge you a bigger fee for sourcing this type of product. You really have to study the numbers to ensure this product works for the property you are purchasing. The benefit of using a bridge-to-let product is that you are able to re-finance quicker than a buy-to-let mortgage. A bridge-to-let allows you to move from the bridging product to the buy-to-let the moment your refurbishment has completed. It usually takes a few weeks for them to process the application and transfer the monies.

What this means is you have your money back within two to three months of completing on the property. If you plan to re-invest this into another property, then it means you can build your portfolio quicker. Due to the expense of a bridge-to-let, it doesn't work on all properties you may purchase.

A sample deal analysis for bridge-to-let is available on www.thebranteffect.com/resources.

Refurbish-To-Let

There's another mortgage product called refurbish-to-let. This is a fairly new product with currently only a handful of lenders offering it. This product allows you to pull your money out even quicker – in around four weeks of purchasing the property, depending on the lender. It's very similar to the bridge-to-let but used for light refurbishments, which is perfect for the C.A.T.C.H.E.R model, as it is using a bridging loan to purchase the property and then it converts onto a buy-to-let.

The lender will ask you to complete a scope of works for the property. They want to see what work you are going to do, how long it will take and an estimate of the costs involved for the work. You are basically detailing your refurbishment plans for them to review. A sample document is available on: **www.thebranteffect.com/resources**.

When the lender goes out to value the property they will value it in today's condition, and also complete a valuation on the post-refurbishment condition of the property, the end market value, based on your scope of works document.

They will then complete a report and send it back to the mortgage company. So, they have valued it today, in its condition today, and they've also valued it with its end value in mind depending on the works that you're going to do for it.

The mortgage company then give you two mortgage offers: one mortgage offer to complete on the property immediately and the second mortgage offer based on its new market value post-refurbishment. So, there is no risk here. Before you purchase, you already know how much of your investment money you are going to be able to pull back out again. How? Because they've given you a mortgage offer already.

Your Key Points:

Money is everywhere.

Use No Money Down Strategies such as: Bridging Finance, Lease Options, OPM and JV's.

Three key mortgage products for building your portfolio: Bridge-to-Let, Refurb-to-Let, Buy-to-Let.

Your Action Steps:

Which No-Money or Low-Money Down Strategy will you use?

Answer: _____

Download the Finance Finder document to define your finance strategy for building your ideal lifestyle at:
www.thebranteffect.com/resources.

BFF-RRR

F - FIX UP

Buy, Finance, and now the next F in the BFF-RRR model is for fix up. A typical refurbishment requires cosmetic updates. You're adding value by improving the kitchen, bathroom, painting, replacing the carpet and tidying up a few bits and bobs. I say bits and bobs, because each property is different.

Kitchens never cost as much to improve as you may think. Have a look at this kitchen below.

It's rather cramped with the small island sticking out into the floor space. It's also dark, has a small sink and feels a little tight in space.

Now, have a look at the kitchen after we had completed the renovation.

We moved that breakfast bar from the centre of the room and placed it along the wall on the left-hand side. We added in a new wall unit and one new base unit. Then, all we did was replaced the kitchen doors and fitted new door handles and re-tiled the kitchen. We kept with a black and white theme as it fitted the property it was in. We also added a new cooker, hob and extractor fan, put new lino down on the floor and replaced the worktop along with the plinths and the cornices, and then painted the room. I needed an electrician to fit the oven, hob, extractor and update some electrics in the kitchen too.

Most of the time when you purchase a property, the units are in good condition so all you actually need to replace are the doors for the kitchen. I have one property and those kitchen units have already lasted 15 years and they're still going strong. This whole transformation you can see cost £1,774.99 and I did none of the work myself. In fact, my DIY skills are absolutely useless so I never do any of the work. I employed a builder to do all this.

The kitchen units and doors I purchased are off-the-shelf at B&Q, not something ordered in (because if you forget one door or you change the design slightly then you have to wait until the new items have arrived, which delays the renovation and delays getting it rented out and money in your back pocket). The off-the-shelf range I use is either the White Country Style or Sandford Ivory Style kitchen range, (this one is the White Country-Style kitchen). They both look great, are of good quality and are sensibly priced. The handles I tend to buy from Amazon because they're a lot cheaper than any home depot store. The kitchen tiles in this picture are also from B&Q and are around £12 per square metre. I've found the specialist tile companies are very expensive in comparison. The cooker, hob and extractor fan I buy from Curry's, Screwfix or B&Q – whoever has the best deal on at the time and can deliver straight to the site for the builder. If the builder can get things cheaper, then I let them sort it out; if they can't, then I show them the price I want to pay for these items and let them collect them or order them online. Don't get involved in ordering or collecting them, because if anything goes wrong with the order you have to get involved in resolving it. It's much better to have the builder order all the parts and deal directly with the companies for deliveries, collections and any problems. This is what you're paying your builder to do.

Here's a breakdown of that kitchen renovation. A full, more colourful case study is available on **www.thebranteffect.com/casestudies**.

Parts	Costs
Worktop – 28mm. 6 metres.	£84.00
Kitchen Units, Doors, Cornice and Plinths	£308
Tiles, Adhesive and Grout	£140.00
Door Handles x 10	£13.99
Oven, Hob and Extractor Fan	£329.00
Labour Fitting Costs (Including Electrician)	£900.00
TOTAL COST	£1,774.99

Bathroom

A typical bathroom renovation also doesn't cost all that much. Here's a before and after picture of the bathroom in exactly the same property.

It doesn't look too bad really, but it does look a little old, plain and dated. Now, have a look at the after photos and see if you can spot the difference!

Now, it's fresh, modern and has added value to the property. We were able to keep the bathroom suite, which nine times out of ten happens: the sink, the toilet and the bath were all in very good condition. We had to re-plaster some of the walls. We re-tiled the whole bathroom, added new taps and a new shower along with a screen and had a new floor and lino put down.

These bathroom tiles are also from B&Q. I can always find good quality tiles for less than £20 per square metre in B&Q. I want hotel quality, so I never buy the cheap stuff. This helps obtain the full market value when you refinance the property and the full market value for the rental income too.

If I need a new bathroom suite, then I jump online and show the builder what I want and the maximum price I want to pay. If they can't get it any cheaper, then I ask them to order it online from Better Bathrooms, Victoria Plumb or Screwfix as they tend to have the best quality at the right price.

Parts	Costs
Bathroom Tiles, Adhesive, Grout & Edging Strips	£312
Sink Taps	£44.99
Floor Re-boarded and Lino Fitted	£90.00
Other Materials; Plasterboard, Plaster, Screws, Paint	£120.00
Labour Fitting Costs (Including Electrician)	£750.00
TOTAL COST	£1,316.99

I have put together a full detailed case study, for both the bathroom and the kitchen, on **www.thebranteffect.com/resources** which will show you in detail the items that I tend to use.

Watching transformation becomes addictively motivational.

Then, in the same property, I had it painted from top to bottom: all the ceilings, walls, doors, the front and the back of the property, which cost £647. I go for natural colours so that it appeals to as many renters as possible. I avoid using magnolia paint as I feel it has started to look a bit dated. Recently, I have used Egyptian cotton with white woodwork as it goes very well together. I recommend lighter colours to make the rooms feel spacious, open and light.

I had new carpet installed throughout the property, with lino for the kitchen and bathroom as this is cheap to replace. I avoid putting ceramic tiles on the floor as if one breaks or gets damaged, and you replace it, then the new tile stands out as the others fade over time. I always use lino as it is cheap to replace the whole thing. This was a total of £583 for the carpet and lino.

This is what I would call a typical refurbishment and everything was done for £4,480.

Most of the refurbs I've done have all cost between £4,000 and £5,000 and I'm not doing any of the work myself; I'm paying for the work to be done. I employ tradespeople to do everything. You'll also have to get a gas safety certificate done annually and an electric safety certificate done every five years. I pay £60-£80 for a boiler service and a gas safety certificate, and £100 for an electric safety certificate.

I work with local builders who are charging around £120 to £150 per day and they give me a fixed price for the job. These builders normally have around five to 10 years' experience in the trade, they're self-employed, but they're not part of a large building company as I've found they charge a lot more. They also aren't big enough to be VAT registered, so

I am not paying 20% VAT on top of their day rate. I talk openly with builders about their day rate and labour fees and will only work with builders that are transparent about them. Some builders will give you a price for the job, but I ask every builder to break that down to material costs and labour fees for transparency. This ensures that I am not being overcharged in either category and also that I work with people who are open, honest and transparent. Money is always the subject that you can test someone's character on. There are builders that will charge more, but I get great value and great quality for around £120 to £150 a day.

BFF-RRR

R – RENT

R is for rent, finding the perfect tenant is critical for success. Prior to making any purchase, you need to ensure that there is a demand for the type of property you are considering buying. You also want to have the biggest possible tenant pool. The more people your property appeals to, the larger the tenant pool you have that will be interested in your property.

I failed at this for one of my purchases. I found a property that fitted the C.A.T.C.H.E.R model. I was able to purchase it 30% below end value, but I got emotionally attached with this property because it is a beautiful penthouse apartment in a Grade II listed building overlooking a canal. It is absolutely stunning.

Because I got emotionally connected with the property, I forgot one key aspect and that was researching the tenant pool. You see, this property is a penthouse. It's on the third floor – the top floor – but it has no lift. It's not a cheap property to live in, but it gives you a fantastic lifestyle.

Therefore, what I found when I tried to rent it was that younger people and younger families are not interested in it. It tends to be someone in their 50s or 60s who are most interested. However, most of those people are not happy with the amount of stairs that it takes to get to the penthouse because there is no lift. It is critical that you test market demand for each property to ensure you will be able to find the right tenant and quickly. I do this by speaking with a number of agents and ask what type of property is in demand, what rents quickly, and what doesn't.

How Will You Know The Rentable Value For The Property?

To begin with I would suggest speaking with three letting agents and asking them how much they think the property is worth on the rental market. I also would search regularly on Rightmove – looking for similar properties, in similar streets nearby, and keeping a note of their rental prices. Estate agents do this all the time; they're looking for comparisons against your property and they're using those comparisons to help decide the rentable value of yours.

Just before you put your property up on the rental market, have a look at what your competition is and what it is priced at. Look at the size, the location and the finish of the property. When yours is live, this is exactly what your future tenants are going to be looking for. If you position it at £25 a month more than the others, you'll need to be able to justify why. Has it got a bigger garden? Is it bigger in size? Has it been finished to a higher standard? Is the location better? You'll need to be able to align your price with the competition.

The Letting Agent Approach

I have worked with a number of letting agents and some are good and some are absolutely awful. I remember this one property that I had with a particular letting agent. They called me to say that the tenant had phoned to tell them that the heater in the bathroom was no longer working. So, I asked them what they suggested we should do about it.

They told me they had already sent an infographic to the tenant helping the tenant to understand how to bleed the radiators as part of the gas central heating. They said that the tenant couldn't understand it. So, therefore, the letting agent's solution was to send out a gas safety engineer and they wanted to charge me £70 plus VAT to do so. This was the first time I had used a letting agency and I was a little bit sceptical about the fact that I was having to make the decision and it was going to cost £70. So, I decided I would speak with the tenant myself and arrange a time to go around.

I went round to see the tenant at the property. The property has *electric* heating – so sending an infographic of how to bleed a radiator, which is part of a *gas* central heating system, was absolutely pointless. The letting agents should have known this because they've seen the property and they've rented it out. So, I went to the bathroom to have a look at the heater that was not working. I noticed just outside the bathroom was a fuse switch. I opened it up and saw that the fuse had gone. Luckily, I had a fuse in my car and so I was able to replace it. It cost me 20p and the heater now works.

What I Look For In A Letting Agent

I look at the size of the company and their approach to viewings. Do they have one person who does all the viewings or is there a team of people? Do they try to do one open viewing and tell prospective tenants that this is the only time they can view the property, or are they available to do viewings to fit around prospective tenants' schedules?

Open viewings are great as they create competition. However, not all potential tenants are free at the time and date set by the open viewing. Therefore, you're missing out on a proportion of your potential tenant pool.

I also look at how they treat tenants – as people or as profit. Do they genuinely care about the tenant and keeping them happy? When you're renting a property, I believe you are not just providing a good home for someone to live in, but you also need to provide a good service. So, how responsive are they to tenant enquiries? What process do they have in place for an out-of-hours emergency? How and when can tenants contact them?

Of course, you want to look at their fees too. What are they going to be charging you and what cost will they charge the tenant? I won't use a letting agency if I think that they're ripping off me or a tenant, because that will affect my reputation. Ask the letting agent how often they inspect the property and how and when they report to you. I have found that it's best to inspect the property often because you'll be able to see smaller problems sooner and deal with them before they become bigger problems. I've found a lot of tenants feel that they're bothering you with maintenance issues and so they just leave the small items. Some fear the landlord will kick them out if they complain, and I hate that because it's my role to provide quality accommodation and they're paying for it to be maintained to the same high standard it was when they moved in.

THE DIY APPROACH

You can choose to take the DIY approach to letting. I have decided to self-manage my portfolio, but to put in place the right systems and automation. My time is very important to me and I don't want phone calls about problems when I'm out with my family. I want to be able to be present in that moment with my family, but at the same time I want to be able to provide a quality service to my tenants. As I've already told you, my DIY skills are awful. My knowledge about boilers, radiators, gas, and water problems is fairly poor as well. So, if a tenant phones me with a problem, I personally can't fix it – I'm useless. So, I empower my tenants. I've created a maintenance and emergency document, which you can download from **www.thebranteffect.com/resources**. This document explains what the tenants need to do in an emergency. I direct them to the person who can help them – the gas engineer or the qualified electrician – and they can phone them directly to resolve the issue.

For non-emergencies, I have an e-mail address and a local telephone number, which is a voicemail that is then converted to an e-mail. I check these e-mails during the day and I forward them on to the relevant tradesperson to resolve. For the things outside of the ordinary, or if I don't know a tradesperson to fix a problem, I have a virtual administrator and so I forward the message to them and they resolve the issue for me, keeping the tenant and myself up to date. This approach means that I can ensure tenants are getting a quality service, but at the same time it doesn't take up too much of my time. Systemising and automating the process really helps.

To find a new tenant yourself can be labour intensive. I recommend finding a local person who can do viewings for you, and a virtual administrator to manage the administration. You may find a local person who is suitable for both the administration and who can conduct the viewings. You may want to do this yourself to see the potential tenants, but I certainly wouldn't do this yourself in the long term. I have a viewing representative find the tenants, but I then have a call or skype interview with them to ensure they are right for the property before we go through the expense of credit and reference checking them.

I would begin your search by looking through a couple of freelance websites. Peopleperhour.com and fiverr.com are good and they have hundreds of people looking for freelance work. What you are looking for is an experienced property administrator, someone who has worked in and around property, as they can help you set up the right systems and processes from the very beginning. Also, test a new person with a couple of small tasks to see if you enjoy working with them. Are they responsive enough? Do they solve problems for you? I've found that some are very high maintenance and require me to keep chasing them, or the quality of their work output is average or poor. If you can trust them with the small things, then you can trust them with the bigger things.

If you find one local person who can do both the administration and be the viewing representative, then this will help. I, however, have found this challenging, so I have a local viewing representative and a virtual administrator and I divide the tasks between them.

I have the virtual administrator place the adverts onto www.openrent.co.uk which then puts the advertisement for your property on to Rightmove and Zoopla. Then have the virtual assistant coordinate with the local viewing representative to do the viewings on the property with tenants. It's essential that your viewing representative knows everything about the property. Make sure you talk them through the refurbishment you did on the property, and give them as much information as possible so they can sell it to the prospective tenants.

When advertising online, you have to ensure that your advert attracts the right tenants. Good quality photos are really important. You can either hire a professional photographer to take them, or train your local viewing representative to take quality photos. The photos are likely to be taken after the refurbishment, which means there is no furniture in the property. I've never had to stage my properties with furniture as there is a high rental demand. However, I do ensure there is plenty of natural light in the pictures, they show as much of the room as possible, and that the property is clean and tidy when the pictures are taken. If there is a difficult room to photograph, then I take a couple of pictures so people can see it from a number of angles to show the size of it.

For the content of the advert, it is important to give as much detail about the property and the area as possible. Don't assume anything. People may not know how close to amenities the property is. Describe the property, the layout, the recent refurbishment, the street and the area the property is in. Paint a picture of the area and the property. Remember you're selling the property: this is your shop window of your product and your service, so make sure you explain that in the advert.

Once the advert is live, you will have people express an interest to view the property. I noticed that around 40% of people did not turn up for their viewings. This was costing me money, so I implemented one thing in the process and that has now seen a 95% attendance rate for all viewings.

We now ask for more details about the person or people wanting to view the property, rather than just scheduling a viewing for anyone and everyone. What I found was those who were genuinely interested responded to our request and those who weren't didn't. We simply ask for details about who will be living in the property, the financial income of these individuals and their previous rental history.

Your virtual administrator will schedule the viewings with your local viewing representative who will show the tenants the property and at the same time assess each prospective tenant. There are two important things that I look for in tenants: firstly, can they afford to live in the property, and, secondly, will they look after it? The first is easy to test, whereas the latter is more subjective and your gut will tell you.

I request from prospective tenants information on who will be living in the property (including pets), and the financial income of those people. I look at affordability in a simplistic way: their rent needs to be a maximum of 40%-45% of their financial income from all sources (such as DSS, employment, or self-employment). This is just a quick calculation as all tenants will go through a professional credit check to check affordability. I also want to know the history of that income to ensure it's secure for the future. How long has that income been coming in for? If employed, how long have they been with their employers? If under six months, then they are likely to be on a probation period.

If multiple tenants are interested, then I have them all complete a pre-application tenancy form, detailing all the above, and then we select one to go through to complete the full checks. If they fail the checks, then we select another until we have found the right tenant.

OpenRent do all the paperwork for you. They conduct all the checks on the tenants, process the application, give you regular updates, and produce the tenancy agreement for you. You do nothing else after the viewings, other than review the reports they give you. It's fantastic.

They advertise the property and sort out all the paperwork for you, they'll collect the first month's rent, secure the deposit in a deposit protection scheme and complete the contract. It's exceptional service.

SOCIAL APPROACH

Now, you could go down the social approach. You can find tenants by advertising free on Facebook or by asking friends or via word of mouth. However, I've found that you get a much better response through OpenRent than any other channel because most people are looking on Rightmove and Zoopla for properties to rent.

Do not be in a rush to find a tenant. It is extremely difficult to evict a poor tenant and it takes months to do it. Therefore, I would rather spend weeks finding the right tenant, than move in someone who may not be able to afford the property, or who may not look after it. I've been a landlord for nearly 20 years, and I have only ever had one bad tenant who left me out of pocket by two months' rent. One of the reasons for this success is because I spend time ensuring we put the right tenants in.

Finding the right tenant is worth waiting for. I have a one-bedroom flat, which is quite a small one-bedroom flat, and I remember having many people interested in it, but none of them passed the pre-application checks. So, I waited and waited for three weeks and then this one lady came to view the property and she was looking to downsize from her current home. She wanted something on that side of town because it was close to work and she fell in love with the property. She was a tenant worth waiting for. I know she will look after that property and I know that she will be in there for years to come. It's worth waiting for the right tenant and not rushing in and ending up with the wrong tenant.

BFF-RRR

R- REFINANCE

There are a number of products on the market that allow you to refinance. Some are quicker than others, as we discussed earlier. The refinance part is very easy. You simply contact your mortgage advisor, who helped you to secure the mortgage in the first place, you let them know that you're looking to pull out your money and they will process all the paperwork and contact the lender.

It will depend on the product you choose – a buy-to-let, a bridge-to-let or the refurbish-to-let, etc. – when you will be able to action this. The latter two are the quickest as you are able to re-finance as soon as the refurbishment is completed. If you purchased the property with a buy-to-let and you are looking to do a further-advance or second-charge mortgage, then you will need to apply for that after you have owned the property for exactly six months. Put a reminder in your calendar to contact your mortgage advisor a week before that, so you can get all the paperwork ready to submit on the day you have owned the property for six months. Obviously, the sooner you can release your funds, the sooner you can move on to the next stage and repeat the process.

Whichever product you select, the mortgage company will want to come out and revalue the property or to check you have completed the works you said you were going to do. If you used a bridge-to-let or refurb-to-let then you've already had the post-works valuation. If you have a buy-to- let then you don't yet know what they will value the property, post refurbishment. This is where your initial research of the end market value is critical. If you're expecting the new valuation to be £120,000, you want to ensure that there are enough comparable properties in the area to prove that is what it's worth.

If you've used a buy-to-let mortgage, then I usually put together a small pack ready for this refinance and valuation as this is such a critical stage in the journey. It includes before and after photos of the property to prove that the work has been done and to show the drastic difference. I also include a scope of works which gives every last detail of the work we have done to improve the property. I also include the comparables of the property that I found before I purchased it, and any more that I have found since I have purchased it.

Now I never want to teach a surveyor how to do their job, but I just explain that I have this information and I'm not sure if it's any use to them but here it is anyway. Most of the time they will take that pack from me. I'll never know if it will impact their decision on the revaluation, but I will continue to do it.

Once the valuation has taken place, they submit their report to the mortgage company, which is normally done within 24 to 48 hours. The mortgage company will then process your application and forward the money to you. This whole process usually takes four to six weeks from beginning to end. It is sometimes faster, but it all depends on the mortgage company.

ASSESSING THE PROPERTY DEAL IN FULL

Now we've talked through the whole process, let's put some numbers together and go through how you assess a property deal and know all the numbers are going to stack up. Head over to www.thebranteffect.com/resources to download the Excel evaluator deal analyser.

When I'm searching around for a property there are a few numbers I want to know:

1 – Its current asking price and any history of its asking price.

2 – Its end value. What do you think this property is worth when you have added value to it? Obtain evidence for this through the Government website and Rightmove.

3 – The rentable value. Search through Rightmove, including already-let properties, and estimate what you think the rentable income is going to be.

Here are the numbers from that one-bedroom flat I purchased last year.

Current Asking Price	£65,000
Potential End Value	£85,000
Rental Value	£450 per month

4 – The cost of mortgage. I want to look at roughly what the mortgage will be on an interest-only basis. We don't necessarily know the number we're going to secure the property for, so at this stage it's just a close estimate. I use the asking price and then when I have viewed the property, I work out what my offer price should be. Then, I cross reference the two.

Here's how to quickly work out the interest-only mortgage cost for any property. Input the purchase price into a calculator then minus 25%, which is the deposit, and this will give you your mortgage value. Times that number by the interest rate you believe you'll obtain on a mortgage.

For example, at the moment you can obtain a buy-to-let mortgage at around 2% to 2.5% easily. So, times it by 2% or 2.5%. Make sure you hit the percentage button. This now gives you the annual interest you will have to pay on a mortgage of that value. Divide that number by 12 and this will give you your monthly mortgage figure on interest-only.

That's purchase price minus 25% times the mortgage interest rate divided by 12. Here's an example

Purchase Price £55,000	Minus 25% Deposit	= £41,250 Mortgage
£41,250 x 2.5%	= £1,031.25 per annum	Divided by 12 = £85.94 per month

I also look at what the monthly interest rate will be post the refinance. For example, I purchased the flat for £55,000, but I refinanced it at a value of £85,000. I want to know what the longer-term monthly mortgage payment is going to be. I would use both the purchase price of £55,000, but also the revaluation price of £85,000, in order to know what the long-term profit is going to be for the property. Also note that when you're buying a flat that there is going to be a ground rent and service charge, so it's important at this stage that you know these numbers and build them into your calculation.

Re-finance Value £85,000	Minus 25% Deposit	= £63,750 Mortgage
£63,750 x 2.5%	= £1,593.75 per annum	Divided by 12 = £132.81 per month

For this property, I now know that the mortgage will be £85.94 per month until I re-finance and then it will go up to £132.81. The rental income is £450 per month, so the monthly profit will be £364.06 dropping to £317.19 after the re-finance.

5 – Then I'm going to want to know what the refurbishment cost is. Now you haven't been to see the property at this point, so you don't know the costs. I can tell you if you follow the C.A.T.C.H.E.R. model and focus on properties that just need cosmetic refurbishments, then the average refurbishment cost will be around £4,000 to £5,000.

Head over to **www.thebranteffect.com/casestudies** to see a number of recent property deals with the exact cost of a number of refurbishments.

6 – The stamp duty will also need to be included and that is at 3% of the purchase price. You'll also want to know the solicitor's fees, which I've found are always around £1,200 per purchase. The other number I'm going to want to know is the mortgage advisor's fee, which tends to be around £300 to £500.

When you have all these numbers, you can work out what the purchase price needs to be. A quick calculation is end market value minus 25%, minus the stamp duty, solicitor's fees, broker's fees and the renovation costs equals your maximum purchase price. To make it easier, I've put a spreadsheet together for you to follow. You can download the Excel evaluator deal analysis spreadsheet from: **www.thebranteffect.com/resources.**

End Value	£85,000
25% Retained Equity	£21,250
Renovation Costs	£5,000
Stamp Duty	c£1,800
Solicitor's Fees	£1,200
Mortgage Advisor Fees	£500
TOTAL	£29,750

For the above, you know the maximum offer would be £85,000 minus £29,750 = £55,250

Now you know the numbers for the property, you need to learn the art of negotiation. When I'm working directly with the estate agent, I want to obtain a picture of why the vendor is selling and what their situation is. We will need to determine if they're a highly-motivated seller. I also want to explain the benefits of selling to me. The main benefit is that of speed and a guaranteed sale, so remind the estate agent that you have nothing to sell, there is no chain, which means you can complete quickly, you have your solicitor and mortgage advisor standing by, so you'll be quick to get the finance and conveyancing completed.

I'll never start with my maximum purchase price because an estate agent is paid on a percentage commission most of the time and they also want to show the vendor that they can negotiate and get a better deal from you. So, I always start *under* my maximum purchase price with the goal of ending at that figure. Don't be embarrassed if it's a low offer. If your first offer through the estate agent gets accepted, then you know you didn't offer low enough to begin with. Explain the work you need to do to the property in order to rent it out and explain what you feel it is worth for you. I personally always ask if there are other parties interested as I'm not going to get into a bidding war. I also ask if any of those parties are first-time buyers or not, as I don't want to take a potential property from a first-time buyer or push up the offer amount for them.

If you are dealing directly with the vendor, or if you arranged to do the viewing directly with the vendor, then make sure you ask the one most powerful question, "What do you need for the property?" I always close in the same way, whether it's with the estate agent or with the vendor, "If I could offer that amount or if I could increase my offer to that amount, would you – or would the seller – accept?" You then know if you do this that they will accept. Don't be in a rush to close the deal. I've had negotiations go for minutes and others for months. Be firm and stick to what the property is worth for you.

BFF-RRR

R – REPEAT

Now you have been through the process once, you will have: your initial deposit back in your hand, 25% equity in the property that you've just purchased, and passive income coming in to you forever. Now you simply use this money and repeat the process over and over again. You recycle your cash through the next property and follow this process: BFF-RRR. Until you hit your goals of being mortgage free, hitting your minimum monthly financial freedom figure, then your financial independence figure and finally your financial opulence figure.

Your Leadership Team

To succeed in property, you are going to need your own leadership team: people who you hire for various services. I've learnt that it's just not worth my time to learn to do everything. It's far more efficient to use other people's time to complete all tasks. These are the people I have in my leadership team:

- A mortgage advisor;
- A solicitor;
- A builder;
- A maintenance team / a handyman who is willing to do those smaller jobs;
- An accountant;
- A mentor – this doesn't have to be an expensive course that you go on. This can be someone you follow online, listening to their podcasts and reading their books and blogs, although I would recommend a 1-to-1 mentor to help guide you through your specific journey.
- A virtual assistant;
- A viewing representative;
- Skilled tradespeople – such as an electrician, plumber and gas

safety engineer.

I would also highly recommend setting up an email which is just to do with property. This will enable you to switch off and only look at messages when you want to, because they're not embedded in your normal email account.

STEP 6 - FIDDLE AND FIX

We've just gone through the first five steps I took to gain financial freedom. The sixth and final one is fiddle and fix. What an earth do I mean? Well, with any strategy, and with a new mindset of move and manoeuvre, you've got to always evaluate, fiddle with things or fix them. Has the market changed and does that impact your strategy? Has new legislation come out and do you have to adapt your strategy because of it? Do you need to fiddle with your strategy or with your formula or do you need to fix something that isn't working?

When the PRA regulations came out, I noticed that my mortgage advisor was really struggling to keep up with my requirements. I sensed that he actually no longer enjoyed the work that he was doing and he had lost his passion for it. I had to fiddle with my approach here and fix it. I needed to make a change to my leadership team in order for my strategy to continue to succeed. I had to fiddle and fix.

As time has gone on, the equity in the properties has increased by pure market growth. My initial strategy had no plan for the increase in equity. I had to ask new questions. Do I re-mortgage and pull the money out? Do I leave the increased equity in there? It's important to consistently review your strategy and evaluate it and fiddle and fix it as things change.

When I first started to build my portfolio, I managed the portfolio myself. I'd do all the paperwork, the viewings, organise the maintenance and I was really hands-on. So, it wasn't really passive income it was actually active passive income. I had to fiddle with that strategy and fix it before it started to take over my life: in effect, what could have happened is that I just replaced the rat race with my own new rat race. What I did was to write down every task I was doing and I looked at how it could be outsourced, delegated, automated or just deleted. OpenRent took a lot of work off me and automated a lot of the paperwork. Having a virtual assistant or two has helped me dramatically. The virtual phone number that I set up also helped reduce my involvement in tasks as this number can be automatically diverted to your virtual assistant.

Your Key Points:

- Kitchen and bathroom renovations rarely cost more than £1,500 to £2,000 each.
- Download the case studies on **www.thebranteffect.com/ casestudies**.
- Ensure your area has a high rental demand by phoning the estate agents and asking them what properties are in demand with low supply.
- Letting agents are good, however the DIY approach can be cheaper and fully outsourced to create pure passive income.
- OpenRent.co.uk will save you hundreds of pounds.
- Your rental has to make a profit immediately, post-finance and on long-term finance (after any fixed rate or discount has ended).
- Property is all about the numbers: purchase price, re-finance price, rental income, monthly mortgage costs, refurbishment costs, professional fees and stamp duty. You need to evaluate the whole deal.
- Your leadership team needs to include: mortgage advisor, solicitor, builder, maintenance team, accountant, mentor, virtual assistant, a viewing representative and tradespeople.
- Allow your strategy to be fluid and adapt to market changes; be prepared to fiddle and fix with your strategy.

Your Action Steps:

1. If you haven't already, then download the Excel evaluator deal analyser spreadsheet from **www.thebranteffect.com/resources** and complete it by finding a property online that's already been reduced by 20%.
2. Go online and find three solicitors by googling conveyancing solicitors in your local area or asking for referrals in a property group on Facebook. Phone and obtain a conveyancing quote from all of them and get one solicitor ready to use on your property purchases.
3. Find a mortgage advisor, using the same method, and talk through what you're looking to do. Have them there ready for you, so when you have an offer accepted, you can say that you've got a solicitor, as well as a mortgage advisor, ready to go.

TAX AND ACCOUNTING

I promise to do my best not to put you to sleep in this section. It's really important to understand what tax implications there are in property. Firstly, I must say that everyone's situation is different, so obtaining full tax advice from a qualified professional is essential. I am not a qualified professional in this matter. However, here are the key things I've learnt in building my portfolio that I hope will help you to start thinking about tax.

Account For Everything

This is essential because if, or when, you have a HMRC inspection you need to be able to prove every expense. Only claim for it if you have a receipt to prove it. I have both a spreadsheet and software, mainly because I can't part with my trusted spreadsheet, but I also realised fairly quickly that software with an app was going to save me a lot of time. I use QuikBooks as I found it to be the least labour intensive and it has some great automation built into it.

With the app you can take a picture of your receipts and it will upload this into the system straight away. You can then code it ready for your tax return there and then. I can do all this in the time that it takes my favourite coffee shop to make my coconut wet latte. You can also set up rules that tell the system that every time it sees an invoice from a particular vendor to always code it in the same way. So, for instance, I only ever have to code my electrician's invoice once, because every time I use him it is for the property portfolio and now the system will automatically code it for me. When you come to do your tax return there are currently six categories to report your expenses in. They are:

- Rent, rates, insurance, ground rents;
- Property repairs and maintenance;
- Loan, interest and other financial costs;
- Legal, management and other professional fees;

- Cost of services provided, including wages;
- Other allowed property expenses.

Your Action Steps:

Start a spreadsheet and, as you build your portfolio, move over to a system. You can download a tax return spreadsheet from www.thebranteffect.com/resources.

Section 24 of the Finance (No. 2) Act 2015

If you purchase a property in your name, or in joint names, you used to be able to claim 100% of the interest charges on the mortgage amount. However, the Government is phasing this out, so you will no longer be able to claim any interest on your mortgage under your expenses if you hold the property in your personal name. The government will instead give you a 20% tax credit for your mortgage interest.

Let's have a look at an example for both a basic rate tax payer and a higher rate tax payer, assuming £600 per month in rent for a property and with an interest-only mortgage of £150. Pretend there are no other associated costs, even though we know that there will be.

You'll pay tax on the full amount of £600 a month x 12 months = £7,200. Your mortgage interest would be £150 x 12 months = £1,800. You will get a tax credit of 20% of your mortgage interest – so that's 20% of the £1,800 = £360.

Rental Income	(£600 Rent per Month x 12mths)	£7,200
Mortgage Interest	(£150 per Month x 12mths)	£1,800
Tax Credit	(20% of Mortgage Interest)	£360
Profit	Profit (£7,200) x 20%	£1,440
Tax Bill	20% of Profit £1,440 – Tax Credit £360	£1,080

A basic rate tax payer will pay profit x 20% which in this case is £7,200 x 20% = £1440 minus the £360 tax credit, means the tax bill for this property is £1,080.

A higher rate tax payer pays 40% tax, so they will pay £7,200 x 40%, which is £2,880 minus the £360 tax credit which means they will pay £2,520. This new approach means the higher rate tax payers will pay more tax for their buy-to-let properties than they used to.

Rental Income	(£600 Rent per Month x 12mths)	£7,200
Mortgage Interest	(£150 per Month x 12mths)	£1,800
Tax Credit	(20% of Mortgage Interest)	£360
Profit	Profit (£7,200) x 40%	£2,880
Tax Bill	20% of Profit £1,440 – Tax Credit £360	£2,520

Now, if you plan to add value to a property, then you potentially have some expenses that you can offset against your property profits.

Capital vs Revenue Expenses

Expenses are divided into two categories – capital and revenue. Capital expenditure cannot be accounted for now; it gets accounted for when you sell the property. Revenue expenditure is claimable in the year the expenses were made. HMRC states that the work taken to bring a rental property to the market is capital expenditure; however, work taken to restore a property to its previous condition, and repair normal wear and tear, is a revenue expense. There can be many grey areas with what is classed as a capital expense and what is classed as a revenue expense. You need to have an experienced property accountant on your leadership team to help you navigate your way through the wonderful process of doing your tax return and allocating these expenses correctly. Getting it wrong can cost you thousands.

SHOULD I BUY IN A LIMITED COMPANY OR IN MY PERSONAL NAME?

If you buy the property in a limited company, then you are able to continue to claim the full amount of interest on your mortgage as a business expense. Very useful if you're a higher rate tax payer. A lot of property investors are now purchasing properties in limited companies and more lenders are offering attractive buy-to-let mortgage products to these limited companies now.

If you're a basic rate tax payer even after you include the rental income from your property or properties, then there may not be any benefit in purchasing in a limited company as you'll get the 20% tax credit which means in essence nothing has changed for you. However, if you are a higher rate tax payer, then there is certainly a benefit of doing so, but it's important to talk this through with an accountant who can look at your situation specifically.

A word of warning – if you are currently a basic rate tax payer, but you are very close to becoming a higher rate tax payer, then the rental income from your property or properties may move you into the higher rate tax bracket, which will then have a huge impact on your tax bill.

If you plan to have your sole source of income come from property, then you may find it tax-efficient to build a portfolio in your own name up to the top of the basic rate income allowance and then purchase all others in a limited company. This will give you more options and flexibility around what you do with the profit from your properties. In the limited company, there are many more tax-efficient options available to you; you can put a tax-free allowance per year into your pension from your limited company, and you can re-invest the profits into further property purchases.

Again, obtain full advice from an accountant who can tell you what works best for your situation. If you are a higher rate tax payer and you plan to continually reinvest all of your property profit into buying more properties, then you'll only have to pay corporation tax. However, the moment you want to draw money out of your business, then you're also liable for dividend tax. You need to have the end goal in sight first before you make any decisions on how best to structure, buy and run your property portfolio.

Mileage and Subsistence

As you start building your portfolio, no doubt you'll be using your car to go to view properties, meet with different people on your leadership team, and go back and forth to the property during the renovation (just because you'll be too excited and you'll want to see it). All of those miles are claimable. Currently, and it hasn't changed for years, 45p a mile for the first 10,000 miles and then you can claim 25p a mile for all miles after that. My software records my mileage for me automatically. All I have to do is tell it which journey was personal and which journey was for business.

You can also claim subsistence; all travel, accommodation, meals and other things like parking, tolls, congestion charges and business phone calls while you're travelling for your property business. Make sure you keep a record of everything. This applies for property viewings but also for any training you do, meeting your leadership team or any networking events that you attend.

Your Action Steps:

To get yourself prepared for building your portfolio, follow these action steps:

1. Find an experienced property accountant, interview them to ensure they have the relevant up-to-date knowledge and ensure they're also an investor themselves.
2. Keep accurate manual and computerised records.
3. Go to **www.thebranteffect.com/resources** and purchase the property tax book I recommend for you to read.
4. Download my Leadership Team document from **www.thebrant effect.com/resources** and complete it.

Other Admin Expenses

Your viewing representative and virtual administrator are part of your business and genuine expenses you can claim. If you are working from home building your property business, then you can claim a proportion of your household costs. Yes, that's a proportion of your council tax, repairs to your home, insurance, mortgage interest, light, heat and so on. All of that can be proportioned to your property business costs. Even genuine business expenses that were incurred prior to your first property purchase can be claimed for, such as your travel costs traveling to view properties, stationery purchases, postage, valuations, mortgage advisor's fees, etc., so it's important to start that spreadsheet now.

THE CHALLENGES I FACED AND HOW I OVERCAME THEM

Everything comes with challenges – and building a life you love through property investment will come with many challenges. I'd like to share with you some of mine. Yes, there were plenty more, but here are some examples and what I did to overcome them. Hopefully, these will help you to avoid making the same mistakes I did.

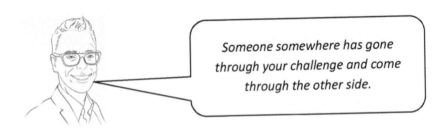

Someone somewhere has gone through your challenge and come through the other side.

Finding The Right Builders

Like every industry, there are good and bad workers. When you are working in property you need to be able to find good builders who will deliver a quality finish. I've been in property for nearly 20 years and in that time I've had some horror stories. Here's what I have learnt about dealing with builders.

- Always get a detailed quote. Ensure it includes full details on what the builder is and isn't going to do, and a total cost. Never begin any job without one.
- Have a plan for rubbish. Ensure it's the builder's responsibility to remove all rubbish from site and that it is done so by a licensed waste management company.
- Agree a payment plan at the beginning of the project. I always pay upon completion of the job and never pay anything upfront.
- Make sure your builder has a trade account set up so they can purchase the materials required for the job.

- Conduct due diligence before hiring a builder. Don't try to give people work just to help them out; give them the work because they are good at what they do and you have got references or you have been referred to them.
- If you smell a rat, stop immediately and start again.
- Don't always believe online reviews.

My biggest lesson in dealing with builders has been that it's important to interview them beforehand, obtain references yourself and only work with people that you get on with and have the right type of character. I found a new builder recently through a newspaper article. I read this wonderful story about a builder who had been out to quote for a job – it was a few weeks' worth of work – to help improve the layout of a house for a disabled child. I read how this builder had moved around his schedule so he could get the work done in time for Christmas so this little girl could enjoy time at home with her family at Christmas. He also decided he wasn't going to charge them a penny for the work he was going to do. I read that article and thought, 'That's the type of builder I want to work with.'

You see, property is a people business and I want to be working with people that I enjoy hanging out with: people that have got the right character, the right morals and the right ethics. So that's now how I find the people to do the work on the properties – I interview them and I start with character. I've also learnt that you need to test them on smaller jobs first, before giving them a larger project. I'll also micro-manage them first. They'll never know *when* I'm going to turn up on site, but they know that I *will* turn up on site. Every other day, I tend to go around and check on each refurbishment that I'm working on with a new builder. Over time, you build a relationship of trust with them and then you can just give them the keys and go around at the end to make sure everything is done. To begin with though, I'm creating some accountability for the builder.

I've found that a multi-skilled handyperson is extremely useful in all refurbishments. There's always going to be the odd job here and there;

like putting up a curtain pole or fixing a door hinge or something small. If you have a multi-skilled handyperson on-site, they're able to do a bit of everything. They're able to jump on to those jobs to get everything done. The best people I've used for refurbishment are multi-skilled tradespeople who are willing to do all the work themselves.

UNDERVALUATION

The biggest challenge which has happened, and I'm sure it will happen again, is when a mortgage company comes out and undervalues the property either at purchase stage or refinance stage.

There's one property I've got and I'll never forget a lender coming out and telling me it was worth £95,000. I had other examples in the street of properties that had sold for £115,000. This was at the refinance stage. So, what do you do? You have evidence that it's worth £115,000, but the lender has just told you it's worth £95,000.

You have two options in that situation:

1. You can argue with the lender and tell them their valuation is wrong.

2. You simply find another lender who will lend you what it is actually worth.

I went for the latter option and I sent out another lender. They valued it at £115,000, the refinance went through and then I could repeat the BFF-RRR process.

Don't run before you can walk; it's stressful.

I remember a time when I had properties I was purchasing, but the refinancing was yet to be done on the previous property. What I was trying to do was get the timing right so that when the refinance happened, the money would come into my account and then I would complete on the next purchase quickly because my goal was to hit financial freedom as quickly as possible.

The problem with that is that it puts unnecessary stress on the transaction. The other thing is that you'll also need some money upfront to pay your mortgage broker fees and the valuations because you haven't had that money come back from your refinance. I was just so determined to gain financial freedom that I would run at a million miles an hour. It was quite hair-raising and very stressful and there were many fires that I needed to put out, so what I would say to other people now is, "Don't add unnecessary stress on yourself by running before you can walk."

Don't put every last penny you have into the deals. Make sure you have structured bank accounts with savings and investments separated. Make sure you always have a contingency fund for properties because sometimes on the refurbishment you will identify problems that you could never have identified when you were viewing the property.

Paperwork Management

When I started out I used to do all the tenancy agreements myself, all the paperwork myself, all the referencing, the inventory reports – everything. This was so time-consuming and a total waste of my time. Now I'm a member of the National Landlords Association. They have a helpline that you can phone about anything. They also have access to every single form you would ever need to use within your property portfolio – templates, tenancy agreements, any notice that you would need for a tenant. Everything you need, they have. For a low-cost monthly payment, you are going to save hours of your time if you join up to the National Landlords Association and they will keep you up-to-date with all new legislation.

Unexpected / Unplanned Problems

Another challenge I hit against with one property that I was purchasing was that they found damp in the interior when the valuation happened. The mortgage company then dictated that they wanted a damp proof report done for the property, which was going to cost £120. The damp proof report said that it needed £1,300 spending on it. Luckily, in this particular deal I had a contingency budget built in place, so even though that extra expense was annoying it was already accounted for. You can never plan the exact figure on a refurbishment cost because you just don't know until you start.

On a couple of properties, the builders have gone to pull tiles off the wall and the whole plaster has come off and then you have to re-plaster. You can never account for that. On another property, the wallpaper was coming off so easily that the painter realised that there was too much moisture and, therefore, damp in the wall that we had to get treated. What I've learnt now is always make sure you have a contingency fund for every project.

Emotional Purchases

We talked earlier about the penthouse apartment that I bought. The biggest lesson I learnt in that is: don't be emotional about a property. Don't buy it just because you like it. Buy it because all of your research says to do so. The other thing about that property is that it's three miles away from my normal area. That's why I didn't check the rental demand; I just assumed it would be strong. Stick to your area, do your research but never get emotionally connected to a property.

Your Key Points:

- Challenges will come; embrace them but go through them.
- Find builders based on references and referrals.
- Don't run before you can walk; it's stressful.
- Expect the unexpected and plan for this.
- If you love a property, walk away. Don't get emotionally connected.

TOP MISTAKES PEOPLE MAKE WHEN THEY START OUT IN PROPERTY INVESTMENT

BUYING THE WRONG PROPERTY

The absolute classic is people getting so excited that they go out and buy a property immediately. The problem is they buy the wrong type of property; they don't follow the C.A.T.C.H.E.R model and so they can't refinance the property and pull their money out. They don't have any more money and so they think their portfolio building days are over. You must have a clear strategy on what properties you are going to buy, how you will add value to them, and when you'll get your money back out.

UNDER-EDUCATED

Another one is that people only research one strategy and then set about implementing it straight away. This isn't too bad, however, it's best to get a good idea of all the strategies out there and then decide which best fits your circumstances. Then implement. I've seen people get bored of the research and due diligence stages and just go out straight away and buy properties. Again, this can land you in serious trouble. People try to do every property strategy on day one. This simply won't work; you're spreading yourself too thinly, having to learn and implement a million different strategies all at the same time. Learn one strategy in detail, focus on it, and become a master of it.

PURCHASING WITH THE WRONG FINANCE

I've seen people purchase properties with the wrong finance. They purchase using a buy-to-let mortgage when actually a bridge-to-let or refurbish-to-let would have been much quicker. Yes, it may have cost a little bit more but you can recycle your money sooner and therefore you'll end up buying more in one year, which ultimately increases your net worth and your monthly cash flow faster.

BUYING PROPERTY IN CASH

One of the top mistakes I see is people buying a property with cash. Let me explain why buying with cash or not buying using the C.A.T.C.H.E.R and BFF-RRR model is a massive mistake, through using an example.

Let's say Joe Bloggs has £125,000 to spend, so he buys a property worth £100,000 with cash and rents it out for £600 a month. He has no mortgage so he's getting £600 profit. That's a 6% yield on his money. With this strategy, he has a property portfolio value of £100,000, with £100,000 equity, and is earning £600 per month.

Property Portfolio Value	£100,000 (Equity £100,000)
Rental Income	£600
Mortgage	£0
Cash Left Over	£25,000
Monthly Profit	£600.00

What is the difference if Joe uses the power of leverage by using mortgages?

Let's say Joe doesn't use the C.A.T.C.H.E.R model; he just buys properties in great condition that he doesn't need to add value to. He can therefore buy four properties all valued at £100,000 each with 25% deposit in each of them. Let's look at the numbers for this. Each property has an interest-only mortgage, let's say at 2%, which is costing him £125 a month. Each rent is £600, therefore, each property is making him a profit of £475. As he has four properties now making a profit of £475 per month, that means he has a total of £1,900 profit a month. With this strategy, he has a property portfolio of £400,000 with £100,000 equity in it and is earning £1,900 a month.

Property Portfolio Value	£400,000
Equity	£100,000

Rental Income	£2,400
Mortgage	£500.00
Cash Left Over	c£3,200
Monthly Profit	£1,900.00

Now let's say Joe had read this book and he uses the BFF-RRR strategy – buying properties and adding value to them. He buys four properties for £90,000 each, he spends £5,000 renovating each of them. His deposit plus the renovation costs are £27,500. Each property is then revalued at £130,000. Joe receives £600 rent per property still, but his mortgage is slightly less at £112.50 a month. So, he's making £487.50 per property, which is a grand total of £1,950 a month. Not much more really, but let's look at his equity and then the potential for his portfolio using this strategy.

Each property has a mortgage of £67,500 (75% of the £90,000 purchase price) but because he used the BFF-RRR strategy and added value they're now worth £130,000 each, which means each property has £62,500 equity in it. With this strategy, Joe has a property portfolio of £520,000 with £250,000 equity, and is earning £1,950 a month.

Property Portfolio Value	£520,000
Equity	£250,000
Rental Income	£2,400
Mortgage	£450.00
Cash Left Over	£0
Monthly Profit	£1,950.00

By adding value, he now has £250,000 in equity instead of £100,000. That's two and a half times more profit by buying properties he can add value to.

Guess what the numbers look like if Joe then refinanced the properties and purchased another four through the BFF-RRR strategy. He would refinance his first four, so they would now have a mortgage of £97,500 (which is 75% of £130,000); the new mortgage figure would be £162.50 a month. So, his profit reduces to £437.50 on those first four properties. He then buys four more, exactly the same as the first four, all at £90,000 all get revalued at £130,000 because he's added value to them.

This is what his portfolio could look like. Are you ready for this? I hope you're sitting down and please don't swear out loud if you're in a public place; it'll be very embarrassing. He would have a property portfolio of £1,040,000 with £380,000 equity in it and would be earning £3,700 a month profit. Isn't that just mind-blowing?

Property Portfolio Value	£1,040,000
Equity	£380,000
Rental Income	£4,800
Mortgage	£1,100
Cash Left Over	£0
Monthly Profit	£3,700 per month

That's why I say to people to educate themselves before going out and buying one property with cash or buying a property that you can't add value to.

Which strategy do you think is best? Buy cash and have £100,000 equity and £600 a month profit or use the BFF-RRR strategy and have £380,000 in equity and £3,700 a month profit? Yes, some of that profit will be used for a letting agent or your virtual administrator and viewing representative to manage the property so you can be totally hands-off and enjoy your pure passive income.

This whole process would take 12 to 18 months.

ANALYSIS PARALYSIS

Another mistake I have seen is people getting so stuck in analysis paralysis that they never actually get started. They spend tens of thousands of pounds and a lot of hours learning all the strategies and going on all the courses and showing off all their knowledge to everyone, but they never actually go to the second step and take action. So many people stay in the cycle of knowledge building because of overwhelm. There are just too many strategies and too many ways of making money in property. This feeling of overwhelm holds them back and stops them from doing anything.

RISK-AVERSE

People don't step out and take risks. I don't believe in taking uncalculated risks, but I do believe in doing your due diligence and taking calculated risks. Remember if you use the new refurbish-to-let product, then most of the risk has been taken out of your purchase. You know exactly how much money you will be able to recycle before you even complete and purchase the property. Your risk has just been dramatically reduced just by using this one particular mortgage.

GIVING UP TOO SOON

People give up just before breakthrough. People overestimate what they can achieve in the short-term and underestimate what they can achieve in the long-term. Property investment is not a get-rich-quick scheme. It took me 22 months to get to financial freedom. We are in a fast-paced world that requires instant gratification. You can't give up when you're on the journey just because you haven't reached your destination yet. Keep focused on the destination, but reward yourself at the milestones so you don't give up halfway through. Don't stop because you hit a barrier. Whatever barrier you come up against in property investment, I guarantee someone else has hit it and found a way around it. I remember when I first had the idea of building a property portfolio, I thought the idea was dead in the water before I even began. I had a pre-conceived idea that you can't get a buy-to-let mortgage if you have no proof of income. I had just gone self-employed, so I had no income, never mind any *proof* of income. I decided to speak with a mortgage advisor anyway and see if there was an alternative plan. He told me that there are lenders that would lend to me without any proof of income. He educated me and informed me that they would look at the project rather than the person. I could have given up before I even started; I'm so glad I made that phone call rather than give up the idea of building a portfolio at the first hurdle due to a pre-conceived idea.

Ensure you're in a community, even a virtual one is extremely helpful. There are many Facebook community groups that share loads of useful information. Networking or having a personal mentor will help you. Don't just stop because it gets difficult. It's not easy, but it's very, very rewarding.

MINDSET

I've noticed that a lot of the obstacles and challenges that stop people from progressing and succeeding are actually all in their mind. Confidence, self-belief, determination, fear, disbelief – they are all upstairs in their mind; so many people have stopped short of success purely because they have let their mind control them. Commit to a millionaire mindset so you can build the life you love through property investment.

FOUR STAGES TO YOUR PROPERTY INVESTMENT JOURNEY

Knowledge Building

Read everything, consume it all, learn as much as you can and have your eyes open to the whole range of possibilities in property investment.

Defining Strategy

You then have to move from knowledge building into defining strategy. There's a massive danger that you stay in knowledge building for far too long and don't move forward into defining strategy all because of feeling overwhelmed. You have to move on to defining strategy and start planning which strategy will work for you. Start with just one and master it, before moving on to another. This will stop the feelings of overwhelm and allow you to focus on one approach which will enable you to move forward and succeed.

Finding A Mentor

As soon as you define what strategy works for you, then I recommend that you start finding a mentor; someone who knows that strategy inside out. Read their book, listen to their podcast, go hang out where they hang out. Find someone who can help you on your journey. Now, I personally never found a one-to-one mentor (other than books and podcasts) so if you don't either, don't let that hold you back. Keep learning but move forward into the final stage, which is the implementation stage.

Start Implementing

You've built your knowledge, defined your strategy, found a mentor or committed to continue your learning. So now start finding a property that suits your strategy and securing it.

FREQUENTLY ASKED QUESTIONS

I've recorded a list of the most common questions people ask me about my journey to gaining my dream life through property investment. Here they are, along with my answers.

Who supported in your journey?

I didn't have a mentor but I did read every book on property I could find and every book on lifestyle and money. My wife and family were my biggest support. My wife was there for me every step of the way encouraging me and pointing out any dangers – like my desire to empty the bank account and invest everything. Ultimately, she kept me grounded and ensured I enjoyed everyday life.

Without my wife's full support, none of this would have been possible. It's essential that you have your partner's total support because there will be challenges which ultimately bring stress or tension into the house. Her calming influence on me and her perspective kept me sane many times. She would always encourage me by helping me to switch off and telling me she had full confidence that I would find a way through whatever challenge came our way. This encouragement, support and empowerment propelled us to succeed. This wasn't a journey I did all by myself: we succeeded because of her support and encouragement and I love her to bits with all of my heart and I wouldn't be where I am now without her.

My sister supported me a lot. Although, she doesn't know it yet, I was able to bounce a lot of ideas off her, pick her leadership and money brains, and she kept me highly motivated because I wanted to prove to her and others that this could be done.

My sister got all the brains and sporting ability from our parents; I was left with nothing! She finished college, unlike me, and got a scholarship to a university in America, where she was the Valedictorian for her year because she obtained the highest grade in the year. She also carried on studying and now has her MBA. She is the smart one in my family, and one of the smartest people I know, so I was able to pick into her brains very often and piggyback on her knowledge to help me build my dream life through property investment.

That support was invaluable so, Laura, if you're reading this (which you'd better be) then from the bottom of my heart thank you so much for all your support. I love you to bits and appreciate your support in helping me build my dream life.

Did you have a bucket load of cash to start with?

I laugh at this question all the time now because as you now know I had −£61.13 and I didn't know anything about building a portfolio of properties or how to do it. I only knew that property made money. I did what I was able to do with the money and income I had, which wasn't massive, then I learnt more. I found a strategy that worked for me and kept doing it.

How did the deals stack up?

I've given many examples throughout the book, so I'll be a little generic here. I made sure that I purchased properties at least 30% below end value. The area I invest in and the best rental return saw me invest in properties between £50,000 and £90,000. I recycled most of my money in every deal, which means each deal was making around 25% profit for me. I've added some case studies detailing all the numbers on www.thebranteffect.com/resources.

With what you know now what three tips would you give your younger self starting out again?

This is a brilliant question. The first thing I would say is that knowledge is power and assumptions or preconceived ideas are from the devil. When I first started investing in property in the late 90s, (yes, I was 19 when I purchased my first property), I had to sell my motorbike and sacrifice a lot in order to get the deposit together.

When I first started out, I was a hit and hoper. I had three investment properties by the time I was 20. However, they weren't the right types of properties to buy. I was lucky because the market was moving rapidly even though I bought the wrong ones. So, if you have read the whole book to this point, you now have way more knowledge than I had when I first started out. Investing in gaining knowledge is critical for success.

Always move forward. Regardless of how small the steps are or how small they feel, do something every day. Listen to a podcast, read a blog, sacrifice a coffee and put the proceeds into your security nest, complete one action step in this book daily, just keep doing something to move forward.

Find a way to build passive income immediately by starting a side hustle.

On average how many hours a week did you spend setting up in the first year?

Well, the honest answer is that I didn't keep a track of it, so this is going to be a little bit of a guess. I have the type of personality that's an all-consuming personality, so I would probably say that I started off quite extreme. I probably invested around 10 hours a week on average but by doubling up my time – for example, by using my train time and my dog walking time to listen to podcasts or reading books. I'd also listen to CDs in the car as well. Then I would start searching for properties on Rightmove while I was on the train or if I was on a long boring conference call at work I might also be on Rightmove at the same time. I'd say on average it was probably 10 hours a week of repurposed time.

What has been the biggest surprise and the biggest disappointment on your journey to financial freedom?

Honestly, my biggest surprise was I actually did it. It was a dream with a strategic plan. I could see that I was moving closer each month, but when that day actually happened – 31st October 2018 – I couldn't believe it. I was shocked. It was a little bit of an anti-climax. I thought,

'Well what now? I don't want to retire and do nothing.' So, I thought, 'I'll just keep going. I'll keep building my property portfolio and now I can start helping others do the same.'

My biggest disappointment is in myself. Why didn't I realise this before I was sitting on the sun lounger in Corfu? I'd been in property and I'd owned property for over 17 years; how come I had never figured this out sooner? I'd say that was definitely my biggest disappointment. I should have educated myself sooner.

What failures did you have in order to get to where you are now?

I think I've failed in almost every aspect of property. I've bought the wrong property at the wrong time in the wrong location with a small tenant pool. I have employed the wrong builders. But every time I've failed, I've picked myself up and kept moving forward. I've never given up because The Brant Effect showed me the life that I wanted for me and my family.

What do you wish you had known at the very beginning when you compare your first property to your last property purchase?

I wish I had researched and understood bridging finance better. There are many more properties that I could have purchased 70% below market value with no deposit, but I missed out on them because I didn't have the right knowledge. Knowledge is power and I wish I'd learnt more sooner.

What advice would you give to someone wanting to start out in property?

First thing I would say is: read this book again. But, joking aside it's easy to let life get in the way of building the perfect life. I highly recommend you allocate time each week, ideally every day, to take one small step forward on your property journey. Never stop learning and always keep moving. Move and manoeuvre. Then decide on the strategy that works best for you based on your circumstances and your personal goals. Take one step towards that strategy each day and each week.

I'm the type of person who learns by doing too, so at some point you have to bite the bullet and just start. Do the analysis but don't get stuck in analysis paralysis. Don't just hit and hope; educate yourself, which you're doing now by the fact that you've read this far in the book. Then move and manoeuvre your way to financial freedom and living your dream life through property investment.

What Are The Next Steps?

Work your way through the four stages of property investing:

1. Knowledge building;
2. Defining your strategy;
3. Finding a mentor;
4. Start implementing.

Set a timeline on how long you are willing to stay in each section for. This needs to be weeks and months, certainly not years.

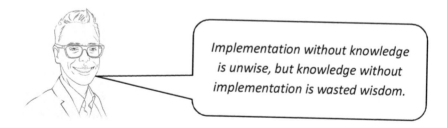

Implementation without knowledge is unwise, but knowledge without implementation is wasted wisdom.

Go back over this book and look at all Your Action Items. I reckon you have probably skipped over some of them or you didn't want to do them at the time you were reading the book, so go back over them and complete those action items, download all the documents and complete them. These documents should help to take you on a journey through to financial freedom.

Make a commitment to learning. The best investment is investing in yourself, so carve out time in your diary to take one small step every day towards your new future.

Seek out a mentor – someone who has travelled the road you want to travel and hold yourself accountable to them or to someone else.

Decide what property strategy is right for you and your current circumstances and make an action plan. Learn everything you can about that strategy online and through books.

Talk to a mortgage advisor if you need one for your strategy and ask them the questions that you want so you can fully understand the financial side of your strategy.

Set a plan and move and manoeuvre.

Recommended Reading

Here are the top five books that shaped my property journey and I'd highly recommend you reading all of them.

1. *The 44 Most Closely-Guarded Property Secrets* by Mark Homer and Rob Moore.
2. *Property Magic* by Simon Zutschi.
3. *Life Leverage* by Rob Moore.
4. *The 4-Hour Work Week* by Tim Ferriss.
5. *The Compound Effect* by Darren Hardy.

Celebrate along the way. This really helped keep me stay focused, but it also helped me to appreciate where I had come from and where I was heading. As the market changes, allow yourself to move and manoeuvre, so adapt your steps. My strategy was always about reaching financial freedom, but the method and journey I took to get there changed a few times.

The end goal doesn't change, but the steps you take to get there may.

Download all the resources you can from **www.thebranteffect.com** and if you want to keep in touch then subscribe to **www.boycottingthenorm.com** which is my blog.

If you still feel overwhelmed and unsure about what your next steps should be, then head over to **www.thebranteffect.com/the12monthplan** and sign up to your 12-month plan to property investment where I've set-up a series of e-mails that will structure exactly what you need to do, month by month, to begin your property investment journey within twelve months.

Let's go on that journey together and yes, it's free!

CONCLUSION

It may have taken The Brant Effect to give me the wake-up call and make me realise the example that had been set for me to follow. But, if I, a college drop-out with two GCSEs, can learn about property investment, implement what I've learnt and gain financial freedom within 22 months, then I know you can too. Yes, it won't be easy but with the tips, strategies and all the resources on **www.thebranteffect.com**, then you have a lot more than I ever had before I started.

Follow the four steps to build your property portfolio:

1. Knowledge building;
2. Defining your strategy;
3. Finding a mentor;
4. Start implementing.

I know you are good enough and I know with the knowledge you now have, you can do it. Keep focused and don't give up. You deserve to achieve financial freedom and to live your dream life through property investment. If you feel you want to know more or need more support in any way, then head over to **www.thebranteffect.com** and let me know how I can help you further on your journey.

It's time to move your dreams into reality.

If I have helped you in any way, then can I ask for one favour? Can you help me to help more people? Can you leave a true and honest review of this book on Amazon, as this will be extremely helpful for others as they consider if they should make the purchase. I want to help get this message to as many people as possible and allow the legacy of my step-father, The Brant Effect, to help people live their dream life through property investment.

Now move forward yourself and use your new-found knowledge to build your ideal lifestyle and live your dream life through property investment.

Notes

Notes

Notes

Notes

Notes

Notes

_____

_____

_____

_____

_____

_____

_____

_____

_____

_____

_____

_____

_____

_____

_____

_____

_____

_____

Notes

Notes

Notes

_____

_____

_____

_____

_____

_____

_____

_____

_____

_____

_____

_____

_____

_____

_____

_____

_____

_____

Notes

_____

_____

_____

_____

_____

_____

_____

_____

_____

_____

_____

_____

_____

_____

_____

_____

_____

_____